THE DALAI LAMA'S LITTLE BOOK OF MYSTICISM

THE ESSENTIAL TEACHINGS

HIS HOLINESS THE DALAI LAMA

Foreword by Robert Thurman
Edited by Renuka Singh

HAMPTON ROADS

D0017328

Hampton Roads Publishing Company, Inc.
Charlottesville, VA 22906
Distributed by Red Wheel/Weiser, LLC
www.redwheelweiser.com

ISBN: 978-1-57174-780-8
Library of Congress Cataloging-in-Publication Data available upon request
Printed in Canada

MAR

10 9 8 7 6 5 4 3 2 1

For All the Seekers

CONTENTS

FOREWORD

The Sakya monk Tenzin Gyatso, the Great Fourteenth Dalai Lama of Tibet, seems to me to be exactly what Sakyamuni Buddha himself would be if that supposedly long-deceased buddha being were to emanate himself back onto this planet, his very own buddha-land called Saha ("The Tolerable"), at this moment in its history. That is to say, the Dalai Lama is fully wise about the realities with which he is engaged; tirelessly compassionate toward all of us suffering beings who are struggling against the seemingly implacable forces of egotism and selfishness that are destroying the viable life-space on the planet; and impeccably competent in his thoughts, words, and physical deeds as driven by the spontaneous and highly sophisticated art that introduces beings to the possibility of their own liberation from suffering.

What was said about Tsongkhapa (1357–1419), the beloved teacher of Gendun Drubpa (1391–1474)—the Dalai Lama's first formally (though retroactively) recognized incarnation in Tibet—can also be said about our Dalai Lama, Tenzin Gyatso (1935–):

> *You are Avalokiteshvara, great treasure of unconditional love, Manjushrighosha, prince of taintless intuitive knowledge, and Vajrapani, Mystic Lord, conqueror of the host of demons—O Tsongkhapa, crown jewel of enlightened sages of the Land of Snows, I bow down at your feet, famously good-hearted Losang Drakpa!*

Once again, I am honored and pleased to welcome a set of eminently useful, pithy teachings of the good friend of us all, H. H. Dalai Lama, skillfully collected and arranged by Dr. Renuka Singh. The best model of the "guru" in Indian and Tibetan Buddhist tradition is precisely the "good friend" (Skt. *kalyānamitra*; Tib. *geway shenyen* or *Geshey*), which emphasizes the fact that we must save ourselves from suffering, with the help of skillful and virtuous friends, rather than merely looking to divine or human authorities to save us.

The bad news for us timid seekers of refuge is that no one, divine or human, however great and powerful, can save us from the seemingly endless sufferings constantly heaped upon us due to our misunderstanding of our relationship to a seemingly alien universe. The good news—and it is really good—is that we are already, beginninglessly, enfolded in the blissful freedom of an ultimate reality that is infinitely abundant in its sustaining energy. So we do actually have the opportunity and ability to free ourselves from our misunderstanding of that reality that causes us to fear and fight and shut ourselves off from its blessings—with the help of the good friends (enlightened beings) who have already at least somewhat transformed their own misunderstanding and fear into wisdom and love.

Among the good friends around today, the brilliant, good-hearted, and competent Dalai Lama stands out as exceptionally effective in his mastery of the art of opening our eyes, expanding our intelligence, and energizing our hearts to see through our confused ideas, discover what is obviously beautiful before us, and arise from our depressed and bitter thoughts of self-dissatisfaction and despair to relate to others in the kind and loving ways that give relief. He himself is a prime example of how joyful a person can be, even in great adversity, as he has been continually beset with extreme mistreatment by powerful enemies, which might be considered sufficient reason to be traumatized, outraged, fearful, and despairing. But here's his secret:

For Buddhists, nirvana, or the true state of cessation of suffering, is the actual refuge. It is our undisciplined state of mind that causes our suffering. If we can eliminate the causes of suffering, we will attain the state of liberation or nirvana, or a true and lasting happiness.

A person becomes a "Buddhist" by "taking refuge." But the Dalai Lama does not seek converts, does not urge people to become Buddhists, out of respect for other religions. However, in this little saying from the work below, qualified "for Buddhists," not to pressure others to agree by fiat, he reveals why he remains happy, no matter how many difficulties he and his people face. He has followed the Buddha's discovery and teaching and has found that reality itself is the "state" of nirvana, freedom from suffering and true happiness—the word "lasting" meaning beyond even pain and death. So just by transforming the mind, exploring reality and discovering its true nature, one finds real refuge from suffering. No need to "become a Buddhist"!

When I think of this little saying, I realize where I learned my shortest answer to the frequent question I encounter: "What is Buddhism?" I always say, nowadays, "Buddhism is just realism!" Since, as a matter of fact, not a matter of religious belief, Buddha discovered that reality is actually the bliss of freedom and love; the more realistic we are, the happier we will be. Some people say, "Ignorance is bliss," because they think reality is frightening and ultimately awful. Buddha and the Dalai Lama say, "Reality is bliss, therefore ignorance causes suffering; knowledge conquers ignorance, and so actually wisdom is bliss!"

The seemingly simple sayings Dr. Singh has assembled, when contemplated over time with a modicum of concentration, overflow with depth of meaning that provides flashes of such wisdom and so encourages your happiness.

The final treasure in the work are the three principles of the path: *renunciative transcendence*— the sure expression of compassion for yourself, letting yourself off the hook of feeling driven to accumulate relationships, wealth, fame, success, etc., so you can focus on life's purpose; *universal compassion for others*—expanding your sense of identification to include others, eventually all of them, and exchanging the misery of self-preoccupation for the joy of loving devotion to others; and, most importantly, the source of such love—*realistic wisdom* that sees through misknowledge and discovers the fortunate reality of things and the courageous and positive attitude it supports.

In sum, the three principles are first, real love for yourself by relieving yourself of clutter and distractions to focus on finding your human purpose in freeing yourself from suffering; second, real love for others, which naturally overflows from your heart when you feel the relief of finding transcendent purpose and you become acutely aware of how intensely most others need that kind of genuine relief just as much as you did; and finally the discovery of the source of all love in reality itself, as revealed to the unerring critical gaze of transcending wisdom that sees through delusive mental habits about the self and the world and breaks through into the blissful freedom that is the reality that you recognize as having always been there for you, in you, and in all others.

So, dear reader, what you have before you in this little book is nothing less than a prescription for improving your life in either modest or far-reaching ways. Tsong-khapa himself famously said, "Of all a buddha's deeds, the deed of speech is the supreme!" Therefore, although the "mystic" may sometimes remain silent in some circumstances, usually out of concern someone will misunderstand her or him, words are vitally important to opening the doorway unto the profound reality that is ever reliable and can be discovered in experience guided by but beyond the words. Therefore, I invite you to open the book and hear therein the voice of the Dalai Lama, contemplate his words, and enjoy his wisdom, care, and humor day by day.

—Robert A. F. Thurman
Woodstock, New York, June 7, 2017

INTRODUCTION

This book consists of informal versions of sayings chosen from interviews with His Holiness the Dalai Lama, his lectures and teachings given at Tushita Mahayana Meditation Centre in Delhi, and a few texts without any identification of the particular sources. The nature and scope of this book is to increase your awareness of the Buddhist tradition and thought that will lead you to a spiritual experience and an existential commitment rather than merely reducing this process to an intellectual exercise. The sayings of His Holiness become fresh and alive in their concreteness and relevance to your daily life. The mystical quest reflected in this work is an integral part of society; thus, it cannot be dubbed as an individualistic enterprise. Human fellowship and equality are aspired to in the context of charismatic authority of love, wisdom, experience, and compassion.

It is abundantly clear from these quotations and lecture that it is only through ethics, concentration, and wisdom, as also reflected in the Three Principal Aspects of the Path—renunciation, bodhicitta, and emptiness—that you tread the Sutric path. You are encouraged not to identify with the impermanent and transient phenomena as you have to delve deeply into the inner core of your existence, which is empty, transcendent, mysterious, and blissful. Acquiring a pure motivation and purity of heart is the ultimate striving, which results in peace and rest in the possession of a sublime *nothing*.

The Greek word for mysticism means to conceal. Mystics, whether theists or atheists, perceive their mystical experience as a part of the project of human transformation. In general, mysticism is best under-stood as a constellation of distinctive practices, dis-courses, texts, institutions, traditions, and experiences that will bring about a change for humanity. Unlike in all forms of mysticism in different traditions, Buddhist mysticism is not typical God mysticism or an experi-ence of oneness with God. Instead, even though the mystical path has an esoteric dimension, one may dare to call it *rational mysticism*, having components that are both philosophical and practical. Buddha, unlike his contemporaries, did not advocate for physical penance, complicated rituals, or prayers that help us to attain the highest spiritual awakening, but it is the disciplined tamed mind that rescues us from our *kleshas*. Also, our fundamental ignorance is responsible for our bond-age to the unenlightened cyclic existence. Hence, we have to cultivate the understanding of the nature of existence, which is facilitated by developing our wisdom. His Holiness the Dalai Lama not only provides a detailed stanza-by-stanza exposition of the Three Principal Aspects of the Path, he also intersperses his commentary with personal reflections and experiences on the practice of his spiritual path.

So, you can see this little book as a treatise of few words, primarily for easy comprehension, which expands the illumination of the wisdom that thoroughly differentiates the relative and ultimate truth of any phenomenon. We hope that this work generates wisdom from contemplating on Dharma rather than gives detailed instructions on practicing Dharma. The exposure of people to Tibetan Buddhism has been fraught with magic and mystery, whereas here we try to highlight the heritage of reasoned analyses and systematic practice.

A basic understanding of Buddhism, especially Tibetan Buddhism, is a prerequisite for understanding the idea of the mystical dimension, both at the philosophical and experiential level. The Buddhist Weltanschauung highlights the fortunate human birth we have with its associated intelligence of the mind. This endows us with the capacity to realize emptiness and achieve enlightenment. The three dimensions of ignorance, attachment, and aversion have to be contended with on this path, whereas ethics, concentration, and wisdom are its markers. Reality is understood at two levels: the ultimate and the conventional level of truth. Ultimate deals with the empty nature of all phenomena, whereas conventional refers to the appearance aspect of the reality. All Buddhist training eventually tries to develop and experience the ultimate level of truth and simultaneously acknowledge the conventional level of karmic existence. Thus, the biggest and hardest challenge we as spiritual practitioners have is to integrate the various aspects of the path (as shown in the quotations and the lecture) into our everyday life by lifting ourselves out of our self-created suffering of negative emotions and attitudes. One needs to develop bodhicitta and compassion, realize emptiness, and achieve enlightenment. This will allow samsara and nirvana to become one. Once you trust and surrender and act on the basis of hearing, meditation, and contemplation, you'll be able to see His Holiness as the Buddha.

Instruction in renunciation, bodhicitta, and emptiness is the foundation for any mystical/nirvanic aspiration. The ultimate purpose of our spiritual practice is to discover the essential nature of our being, which is clear, pure, and blissful. What we see around us is actually nothing more than a projection of our inner landscape. The Buddhist point of view identifies our consciousness as the source of our circumstances. For example, painful and confusing situations or happiness arise from similar states of mind. Enlightenment is achievable, now or later, if only we can get rid of our delusions—attachment, hatred, and ignorance—that cloud our mind and prevent our inner sun from shining. We can adopt a gradual or speedier process to develop qualities of love and wisdom, depending on our tendencies, inclinations, and predilections. This means that we evolve from ordinary and deluded beings into totally conscious beings with immeasurable compassion and wisdom. The supreme motivation of bodhicitta helps us to achieve enlightenment for the sake of all sentient beings. Only by opening our hearts to others can we experience true happiness ourselves. Let us keep in mind that the mystical meaning of the Tibetan mantra *Om Mani Padme Hum* dwells on the fact that once you surrender, you can spiritually transform your mind, matter, and your surrounding environment. The validity of the mystical experience is clearly reflected and visible in the lives of the highly evolved lamas as they generously impart their wisdom while interacting with us. It is interesting to note that there is a great similarity of mystical expressions and vision in most of the religions, even though some differences may exist in their articulation. This manifests in the form of a consciousness that imparts the experience of nonduality, bliss, and purity. It is the "now" moment that becomes an eternity. There is no before, no after, neither this nor that. In perfect simplicity, we experience the eternal stillness, making us act in the freest manner possible.

Let me now quote His Holiness, who has been seen as the most mystical teacher and scholar. He describes Tantrayana as follows:

According to the unique description of highest yoga tantra, Buddha nature is the subtlest mind-wind, whose nature is empty of inherent existence. The subtlest mind is an extremely refined state of mind, also called the inner clear-light mind. The subtlest-wind energy is its mount. The two are inseparable. All sentient beings have this subtlest mind-wind, and its continuity goes on until awakening: it is not a sour or independent essence; it changes moment by moment and is selfless and empty of independent existence. When we die, the coarser levels of mind dissolve into the innate clear-light mind, and when we are reborn, coarser consciousnesses again emerge from the basis of the innate clear-light mind. When these coarser levels of consciousness are present, constructive and destructive thoughts arise and create karma. The result of afflicted thoughts in samsara, the result of virtuous mental states such as renunciation, bodhicitta, and wisdom is the attainment of nirvana. Sentient beings' subtlest mind serves as the substantial cause for a Buddha's wisdom Dharmakaya, and the subtest wind-energy is the substantial cause for a Buddha's form body.

Through special tantric practices this subtlest clear-mind is activated, made blissful, and then used to realize emptiness. Because this mind-wind is so subtle, when it realizes emptiness directly, it becomes a very strong counterforce to eradicate both afflictive and cognitive obscurations. In this way, Buddhahood may be attained quickly. **"**

—His Holiness the Dalai Lama, from
Buddhism: One Teacher, Many Traditions

The Tantric meditations on mandalas and deities might seem mysterious, and you may find them more appealing, but they can be very disappointing, disillusioning, and disheartening as they may not result in any mystical experiences. In this work, we are not focusing on the details of the Tantric path because practitioners maintain that these details should be taught in secret, to suitable students only, who have received the appropriate initiation, and that they should not be commercialized.

As shown in the Sutric path earlier, the secrecy of the Tantric path is not applicable to the practice of bodhicitta. Thus, it is vital that you try to cultivate bodhicitta through aspirational prayers. It is here that the role of the guru gains significance.

So, whether it is the graduated path to enlightenment, the mystical approach of Vajrayana, or the highest yoga tantra meditations, the teachers on this path extol its simplicity in the sense that deep down within yourself, something is touched and transformed. This is accomplished by being inspired by a real master and by having a valid experience of the spiritual realm.

Thus, as Buddhists, we need to take refuge in the three jewels of Buddhism; the four noble truths—the pervasiveness of suffering, its origin, its cessation, and the path to its cessation—the noble eightfold path; the three higher trainings of ethical conduct, concentration, and wisdom; and the four immeasurables of love, compassion, joy, and equanimity. All of us can liberate ourselves on this path by reducing the gap between samsara and nirvana, and by ultimately breaking the cyclic existence fueled by our karmic causation. Even if our practices and contemplations fail to transport us to the state of enlightenment, they can at least free us from the fears of death and dying and give us some amount of control over our rebirth.

I hope and wish that this work will touch the hearts of many and reconnect solitary beings with each other..

—Renuka Singh, December 2016

SELECTED QUOTATIONS

from

HIS HOLINESS THE DALAI LAMA

1.

Even as ordinary people we must try to use this precious opportunity before we die to gain a secure realization of the Dharma, the teaching of the Buddha. If we can do that, we will not have to fear death. A good practitioner can die peacefully without regret because his or her human potential is fulfilled.

2.

Only by working hard and undergoing hardship over a long period of time will we be able to attain enlightenment. It is not easy to attain all the spiritual levels and realizations within a short time without making any effort.

3.

Eliminating negativity and cultivating positive activities is not possible merely by changing our physical or verbal behavior. It can be done only by transforming the mind. In the practice of Buddhism, our goal is to attain nirvana and the state of Buddhahood.

4.

The intrinsic nature of the mind is pure; the disturbing emotions that afflict it are only temporary flaws. However, the negative emotions cannot be removed by the most advanced surgical technology. It can be achieved only by transforming the mind.

5.

External constructions, however well you make them, will crumble and disintegrate. What we create within our minds will last much longer.

6.

Sufferings, like sickness, aging, and death, are problems related to the very nature of our existence, and we cannot overcome them by external conditions. As long as our minds are beset by negative thoughts, even if we have soft, comfortable clothes and delicious food to eat, they will not solve our problems.

7.

Even our birth is accompanied by suffering; we are faced
with sickness, aging, and not getting what we want, and
with encountering situations we do not want. Problems
like work are man-made. But as long as we are born in
the cycle of existence and disturbing emotions envelop
our mind, we will not find any peace or happiness.

8.

If we understand the whole cycle of existence as having
the nature of suffering, we will engage in the practice
of the three trainings: ethics, meditation, and wisdom.
Since it is possible to be liberated from the cycle of existence, training the mind to aspire to Buddhahood is
essential.

9.

For Buddhists, nirvana, or the true state of cessation of suffering, is the actual refuge. It is our undisciplined state of mind that causes our suffering. If we can eliminate the causes of suffering, we will attain the state of liberation or nirvana, or a true and lasting happiness.

10.

We have found this precious life as a free and fortunate human being; sooner or later we have to face death. If we then fall into an unfavorable state of existence, it will be very difficult to find an opportunity to engage in the practice of the Dharma.

11.

It is not enough to be born in favorable states of existence as a human being or a god. As long as we do not tame and eliminate the disturbing emotions in our minds, we will find no occasion to experience joy and lasting peace.

12.

The awakening mind is the intention to achieve Buddhahood in order to free all beings in the universe from suffering. In order to develop the awakening mind, we must meditate; it cannot be cultivated merely by wishful thinking and prayers. It cannot be cultivated merely by gaining an intellectual understanding of what it means, nor simply by receiving blessings. It can be done through meditation and repeated and prolonged habituation.

13.

The awakening mind is a mind with two aspirations. It is a mental consciousness induced by (1) an aspiration to fulfill the purposes of others, assisted by (2) an aspiration to achieve Buddhahood. In other words, it is compassion focusing on sentient beings and wisdom focusing on enlightenment.

14.

The four noble truths help us to reflect on our sufferings and gain the determination to free ourselves from them. The four noble truths can be classified into two categories. The first two truths, true sufferings and true origins, are the set of distressing causes and effects associated with the disturbing emotions and the sufferings that we want to overcome. The second set of two, true cessations and true paths, are the set of causes and effects of the pure category. The last two noble truths reveal a complete path for our future course of action.

15.

Each of the four noble truths can be explained according to four attributes. The four attributes of true sufferings are impermanence, suffering, emptiness, and selflessness.

16.

Causes and conditions create true sufferings in such a way that by their very nature, they disintegrate and change from moment to moment. Therefore, true sufferings are clearly dependent on their causes.

17.

To help our meditation, there are three principal ways to think about suffering. These are the suffering of pain, the suffering of change, and the pervasive suffering that is a condition of existence.

18.

Our principal misdeeds committed under the sway of disturbing emotions are summarized as the ten nonvirtuous actions. Physically these are killing, stealing, and sensual misconduct. Verbally they include lying, divisive talk, harsh speech, and idle gossip. And mentally they consist of covetousness, harmful intention, and wrong view.

19.

Whether we think of ourselves as fully ordained monks, or great tantric practitioners, or simply Dharma practitioners, it is often the case that either our motivation is not good in the beginning, our actual practice of visualization and meditation is not good in the middle, or our conclusion is not good. All of our various practices are interrupted by negative thoughts, so they remain weak and frail.

20.

Only the awakening mind, which leads to enlightenment, has the power to exhaust powerful negative deeds. Even in ordinary life, the mind wishing to benefit other sentient beings is priceless.

21.

One of the principal factors that will help us remain calm and undisturbed at the time of death is the way we have lived our lives. The more we have made our lives meaningful, the less we will regret at the time of death.

22.

If the daily life is quite positive and meaningful, when the end comes, even though we do not wish for it, we will be able to accept it as a part of our life. It is by living in harmony with reality that we will make our life meaningful.

23.

Others are the objects on whom our peace and happiness depend; it is therefore proper for us to take care of them. But we tend instead to think that we have achieved everything by ourselves.

24.

A nonviolent approach is a human approach, because it involves dialogue and understanding. Human dialogue can be achieved only though mutual respect and understanding in a spirit of reconciliation. This is a way to make our lives meaningful.

25.

A compassionate attitude does not mean a mere passive feeling of pity. In a competitive modern society, sometimes we need to take a tough stand. We can be thoughtful and still be compassionate.

26.

Once you have an experience of the deeper subtle mind in meditation, you can actually control your death. In Tantra there are advanced practices such as transference of consciousness, but I believe that the most important practice at the time of death is the awakening mind.

27.

Remembering death is a part of Buddhist practice. There are different aspects to this. One is to meditate constantly about death as a means for enhancing detachment from this life and its attractions. Another aspect is to rehearse the process of death, to familiarize yourself with the different levels of mind that are experienced as you die. When coarser levels of mind cease, the subtle mind comes to the fore. Meditating on the process of death is important in order to gain deeper experience of the subtle mind.

28.

We have to travel to the next world alone, unaccompanied. The only thing that will benefit us is if we have undertaken some spiritual practice and have left some positive imprints within our minds. If we are to stop wasting our lives, we have to meditate on impermanence and our own mortality.

29.

As a result of death meditation, a practitioner becomes less obsessed with the affairs of this life—name and fame, possessions, and social status. While working to meet the needs of this life, someone who meditates on death finds the time to generate the energy that can bring about peace and joy in future lives.

30.

When you are well fed and enjoying the sunshine, you look like a practitioner. But when faced with a crisis, you reveal your true nature. Everyday experience tells us that most of us are like this. A weak awareness of death makes meditators behave like ordinary people in times of crisis, becoming excessively angry, attached, or jealous.

31.

If we could take the lord of death to court, we would surely do so. Yet no military power can capture death. The richest person cannot buy death off, and the most cunning person cannot deceive death by trickery.

32.

With negative states of mind like anger, jealousy, competitiveness, and attachment, we need to understand why they are negative, how they arise in us, and how they leave us disturbed and unhappy. Understanding their drawbacks will help us reduce them.

33.

It is said that the more worldly activities you start, the more there are, like unceasing waves on the sea. Would it not be better just to stop and begin to practice the Dharma?

34.

Traditionally we are advised outwardly to observe monastic discipline, inwardly to meditate on the awakening mind, and secretly to practice the two stages of the path of Tantra. It is extremely important to practice Dharma when we are young, when both body and mind are fresh and energetic. Generally, when people become old, they suffer the sickness of old age, and their memories become weak.

35.

We have displayed indifference toward neutral sentient beings, attachment toward friends, and anger, jealousy, and hatred toward our enemies. We have accumulated negative deeds like these for a long time for the sake of this fleeting impermanent life. The actual refuge is only the Dharma.

36.

Whether sentient beings are critical, sarcastic, or mocking, they are making a karmic connection with us. Therefore we wish that this karmic connection may become a cause for their attaining enlightenment.

37.

When you wage a war with an ordinary enemy, you might gain the victory and drive the enemy from your country. Ordinary enemies can regroup, reinforce, and reequip themselves and return to the battle. But when you fight the disturbing emotions, once you have defeated and eliminated them, they cannot return.

38.

Immature people are those who have little mental or spiritual growth. Such narrow-minded people are like squabbling children who are unable to live together. Do not be discouraged by their lack of contentment. Instead, generate compassion for them, reflecting that the disgruntled expressions of these children are due to the preponderance of disturbing emotions in their minds.

39.

Anger and hostility can cause great damage in this life as well as in future lives. Irrespective of our amiability and politeness, when anger erupts, all our good qualities vanish in seconds. Anger disturbs our own peace of mind as well as that of everyone around us. It creates conflict and unhappiness. It gives rise to coarse physical and verbal behavior that we would otherwise be too embarrassed to engage in.

40.

What fuels anger is frustration when we do not achieve what we want or when we experience what we do not want. Anger is also fueled by mental distress, and that is what we must try to prevent as it always disturbs the mind and does us harm.

41.

There are people who mortify and mutilate themselves under the guise of religion. If people are prepared to undergo hardship for such meaningless purposes, why can't we undergo certain hardships to attain the state of liberation, an enduring state of peace and happiness? We cannot afford to flinch from hardship for the sake of liberation.

42.

It is the nature of the mind that the better acquainted it becomes with doing something, the easier that thing is to do. Suffering viewed from a transformed perspective will help us tolerate even greater levels of suffering. There is nothing that does not get easier with familiarity. If we get used to putting up with minor hurts, we will gradually develop tolerance for greater pain.

43.

The mind is not physical. No one can touch it, no one can harm it directly, and therefore, no one can destroy it. If someone says something threatening, harsh, or unpleasant to you, it does no actual harm. So there is no need to get angry.

44.

Life can be compared to two dreams. In one dream you experience happiness for one hundred years and then wake up; in another dream you experience happiness for only a moment and then wake up. The point is that after you have awakened, you cannot enjoy the happiness of your dreams again; whether you live a long or a short life, you will have to die.

45.

When there is lack of social harmony, remember that sentient beings have different dispositions, different ways of thinking. This is natural. If some agitation, confusion, or disturbance arises, you should be able to see it as a result of your own action and so avoid resentment.

46.

If you want sentient beings to be delivered to the exalted state of Buddhahood, why do you feel distressed when they obtain possessions and respect? If sentient beings find happiness and reduce their suffering of their own accord, it is worth rejoicing about. People who are angry when others prosper have no awakening mind within them.

47.

People who worry about a decline in their name and fame are like those small children who work hard to construct a sand castle and cry the moment it collapses. Therefore, when someone praises you, do not feel too happy. Name has no essence, fame has no meaning. Attraction to name, fame, and respect will distract you from your virtuous qualities.

48.

Patience is extremely important for a bodhisattva, and patience can develop only because of the presence of the enemy. Since our practice of patience is the result of both our own effort and the presence of the enemy, the resultant merit should first be dedicated to our enemy's happiness. Even though the enemy provokes the practice of patience, it was not his or her intention to do so.

49.

If you are able to develop a strong sense of compassion and loving-kindness toward your enemy, you will be able to generate similar loving-kindness and compassion toward all sentient beings. It is like removing a huge stone that has been blocking the flow of water in a canal. Once you remove the stone, the water immediately starts to flow.

50.

While we remain wandering in the cycle of existence, as a result of practicing patience over many lives, we will have an attractive physical form. We will have a long life free from sickness, and we will attain the peace of the ruler of the universe.

51.

We need to make an effort in our quest for spiritual realization. When laziness takes over, our pursuit of the Dharma will not advance. Effort should be steady, like a stream of running water. Effort implies that we take an interest in whatever we are doing. In this context, it is a question of taking joy in practicing the Dharma.

52.

One of the ways to counter laziness is to think about impermanence and the nature of death. Death has no compassion. Gradually one by one, death takes us all. When death will strike is unknown and it can catch us unaware any time. Once death overtakes us, it will be too late to eliminate laziness.

53.

There is a danger of worrying that if you die, who will help you? Who will pray for you? But the Kadampa masters used to think, "Why should I care whether someone helps me or not? I should prefer to die a natural death in a bare and empty cave just as animals and birds do."

54.

When you achieve single-pointed concentration, you can focus your mind on any object. By combining special insight into emptiness with the practice of the calmly abiding mind, you will be able to destroy the disturbing emotions. To cultivate such a special insight, you must first cultivate concentration.

55.

Friends and relatives are not permanent. They change from moment to moment. You destroy the possibility of finding the unchanging state of liberation as you are attached to them. Hence, your own attachment creates and contributes to the development of attachment in others.

56.

It is said that you should live in such a way that all you own is what you stand up in. That means you have nothing to carry and nothing to hide.

57.

The purpose of leaving the household life is not to do business or start a new project or deceive people. The only purpose is sincere spiritual practice. If you do that and do not worry much about your food, clothing, and possessions, but engage mainly in the practice of meditation, the life of an ordained person is just wonderful.

58.

There is a verse that says that if you sincerely practice, even if you stay and lead the life of a householder, nirvana will be yours. But if you do not practice, even if you remain in the mountain for years, hibernating like a marmot, you will not achieve anything.

59.

In meditation there is also a process of cultivation of the awakening mind by exchanging your own welfare for the sufferings of others. You see yourself and other sentient beings as of equal nature. This process is very powerful. It is supported by reason and logic, but it can also be understood in the light of our own day-to-day experience.

60.

When many beads are strung together, we call them a rosary, but like our body or an army, it has no intrinsic existence. The person who possesses suffering is also a designation and has no intrinsic existence. We should be concerned about the sufferings of other people now. Ultimately everything is empty of intrinsic existence; there is no true owner of suffering. Suffering is suffering, and it must be dispelled.

61.

Ordinarily, those worse off than you are jealous, those who are equal are competitive, and those better off than you bully you. In turn, you bully those worse off than you, compete with your equals, and are jealous of those better off than you. Cultivate a fresh intention to side with sentient beings and denigrate your old self. Be jealous of your old self, be competitive with your old self.

62.

Under the sway of self-centeredness from time immemorial, you have brought yourself only harm and suffering. Now take control of this misplaced attitude and destroy it. If your mind does not comply, the only thing you can do is destroy your self-centered attitude.

63.

A Buddha possesses many physical, verbal, and mental qualities, but here the Buddha is being hailed in terms of wisdom, his precise realization that the meaning of emptiness, dependent arising, and the middle way are synonymous.

64.

We cannot accept a teaching literally simply because it has been taught by the Buddha; we have to examine whether it is contradicted by reason or not. If it does not stand up to reason, we cannot accept it literally. We have to analyze such teachings to discover the intention and purpose behind them and regard them as subject to interpretation. Therefore, in Buddhism, great emphasis is laid on the importance of investigation.

65.

When we search for the meaning of truth, we are searching for reality, for the way things actually exist. Whether we are dealing with external or internal phenomena, it is important to understand their mode of existence and how they function. This is called the *logic of suchness*, which means that we investigate things on the basis of their suchness or nature.

66.

All Buddhist schools of thought accept what are known as *the four seals*: all phenomena are impermanent, all composite things are in the nature of suffering, all phenomena are empty and selfless, and nirvana is peace.

67.

Different categories of the mind, like attachment and hatred, are based on the mind's misconception of things as having objective existence. When we cultivate a mind focused on selflessness, it opposes the misconception of the true existence and thus automatically weakens the force of our attachment and hatred.

68.

Whatever appears to your mind appears to have intrinsic existence. This is because our minds are obscured by ignorance. We should be able to understand this, and as a result, know that whatever appears to our minds is due to the power of ignorance and its imprints.

69.

If our practice results in our becoming people without hearts who show no concern for others' peace and suffering, it is not a good practice. Therefore, not only during meditation, but also during post-meditative periods, you should always guard the doors of the senses with mindfulness, conscientiousness, and alertness.

70.

Cultivate strong faith and observe the ten virtuous actions. Avoid wrong livelihood, avoid all kinds of commotion, study and meditate on the meaning of the scriptures, and work for the welfare of all beings in the universe.

71.

Just as the heat of fire is not created by someone else, for it is the nature of fire to be hot, and just as it is the nature of water to be wet, so there is something called consciousness or mind, on the basis of which we have feelings of pleasure and pain. In order to bring about transformation in the mind, first we need to identify what mind or consciousness is.

72.

The darkness of the mind refers to our misconception of self and our self-centered, selfish altitudes, the negative aspects of the mind. Just as the sun's rays dispel darkness, mind training dispels the darkness of ignorance.

73.

If our emotions fluctuate wildly and we are subject to hatred and jealousy from the very start of the day, we will not even be able to enjoy our breakfast and our friends will avoid us. So unstable emotions not only disturb our own state of mind, they also disturb the minds of others. This is why an altruistic attitude brings a great sense of happiness and peace of mind.

74.

The point is that the Dharma practice takes place in our mind. It would be a mistake to think that simply changing our clothes, saying prayers, or making prostrations encompasses the entire practice of the Dharma.

75.

Ignorance, the belief that things exist as they appear, independently and autonomously, without depending on causes, is the root of all delusions. To counteract these ignorant and self-centered thoughts, one needs to generate loving kindness, compassion, altruism, and the wisdom of understanding emptiness.

76.

Rather than being confrontational, it would be wiser and more meaningful to learn from each other. In this way religious people can play a positive role in creating peace and harmony in the world.

77.

In Buddhism, quality, not quantity, is what really counts. The Dharma is not preserved or propagated by force. Buddha expounded the perfect path based on the experience of the awakening mind and the six perfections of generosity, discipline, patience, effort, concentration, and wisdom.

78.

In Buddhism, appropriate teachings are to be imparted to appropriate disciples. Thus, only truly dedicated and spiritually oriented disciples are encouraged to get involved in Dharma. Teaching Tantra is severely restricted, and only selected disciples are permitted to receive it. However, today Tantra has become the subject of popular public teaching.

79.

The person who is constantly working for others, deep down, is free of anxiety and calm. The body becomes a realm of joy, because no external circumstances can disturb that person's presence of mind. The body becomes a conflict-free zone because there is no inner conflict and no external circumstances can be upsetting.

80.

There are four preliminary practices: thinking about the rarity and potential of life as a free and fortunate human being; reflecting on death and impermanence; thinking about actions and their results; and reflecting on the faults of the cycle of existence.

81.

Meditation means creating a continual familiarity with a virtuous object in order to transform your mind. Meditation can be of two types. Analytical meditation uses analysis and reflection, whereas in single-pointed meditation, the mind dwells on whatever has been understood.

82.

To stimulate and increase the power of your awakening mind, meditate on what are called the four immeasurables: immeasurable love, immeasurable equanimity, immeasurable compassion, and immeasurable joy.

83.

It is said that developing faith in the spiritual master is like the dawning of the sun on the path to enlightenment. After you have developed faith, cultivate deep respect by reflecting upon your teacher's great kindness: The most important aspect of this kindness is that he or she guides you on the path leading to enlightenment.

84.

Develop a strong conviction that you have received the inspiration of the spiritual master's body, speech, and mind. There is the eight-petaled lotus of the heart, which refers to the mind, because we sometimes identify the mind with the heart.

85.

There are certain channels in our body, some visible and others very subtle and invisible. When we undertake certain tantric practices involving visualization of channels and focus on the vital points of the body, it has a physical effect. You can visualize the indestructible drop within the channel wheel at your heart. When the spiritual master dissolves through the crown of your head, you should visualize him or her becoming absorbed into the indestructible drop at your heart.

86.

The Tibetan word for inspiration actually means "force of transformation," implying that the various qualities of the object transform the nature of your mind. When we seek blessings, we are also seeking a transformation within our minds.

87.

It is said that at death the best practitioner is delighted because he is changing his form for a better and more suitable one with which to practice Dharma. The middling practitioner has no desires but is completely prepared. And even the poorest practitioner has no regrets about having to die.

88.

Practice during the post-meditation period is equally important. As a result of the inspiration gained during the meditation sessions, we can develop many virtues like compassion, benevolence, and respecting other's good qualities, but the real test is when we are faced with the outside world. Therefore, we must be diligent in our practices during the post-meditation period.

89.

Unless we have some experience of suffering, our compassion for others will not amount to very much. Therefore, the will to free ourselves from suffering precedes any sense of compassion for others.

90.

We may be brave, cunning, and clever, but whatever tactics we use, there is nowhere to escape from death, not high in the mountains, deep in the sea, in the densest forest, or in the crowded city. Even the most spiritually evolved have passed away, not to mention the most powerful kings and the bravest warriors. Everyone, rich and poor, great and small, man and woman, has to die. Our life span is defined by our karma. Prayers for long life and longevity empowerments might enhance one's life to some extent, but it is very difficult to prolong or add to it.

91.

After our deaths, we do not disappear; we take rebirth. We do not take birth voluntarily; we are compelled to do so though the force of our actions. If we are to ensure our future well-being, it is important to cultivate wholesome actions, because existence as an animal, hungry spirit, or inhabitant of hell is extremely miserable. Practitioners aspire to attain a more fortunate rebirth.

92.

The principal way to attain a fortunate rebirth is to abstain from the ten nonvirtuous actions. These ten include three physical activities—taking a life, taking what is not given, and committing abusive sexual behavior; four verbal activities—lying, slander, harsh words, and idle gossip; and three mental activities—covetousness, malice, and wrong view.

93.

Human beings are not intrinsically selfish, because selfishness is a form of isolation. We achieve happiness, prosperity, and progress through social interaction. Therefore, a kind and helpful attitude is the source of happiness. And the awakening mind is supreme among all such beneficial thoughts.

94.

Whether you enter the Sutra vehicle or the Tantra vehicle, the only entrance is with the awakening mind. It is like a field in which to cultivate all positive qualities. It is like the god of wealth who removes all poverty. It is like a father protecting all bodhisattvas. It is like a miraculous vase fulfilling all your wishes.

95.

The mind cannot be transformed by force, using knives and guns. It may seem to be weak, having no color or shape, but it is actually tough and resilient. The only way to change it is by using the mind itself. For only the mind can distinguish between what is to be done and what is to be given up.

96.

You should cultivate the forbearance that is not discouraged when you are harmed or opposed. The more you are harmed, the more you should be able to develop patience and compassion toward whoever is harming you. If you are able to do that, even if you are besieged by antagonists, it will become a source of merit and compassion. Your practice will be like a panacea for all ailments.

97.

Twenty-two kinds of awakening mind have been described in the scriptures. Until you have attained the stability of the earth-like awakening mind, there is a risk of its degeneration. Thus, compassion should be augmented by compassion. Compassion and wisdom should be practiced in combination.

98.

There are two ways to collect virtues. The collection of merit is acquired by generating compassion, love, and the awakening mind. The collection of wisdom is acquired by reflecting on the meaning of emptiness and by generating the wisdom of understanding emptiness.

99.

Even emptiness has no independent existence, so we talk about the emptiness of emptiness. All phenomena are devoid of intrinsic existence. Accordingly, having intrinsic existence by its own nature or in its own right, having ultimate existence, having free existence, and having real existence all mean the same thing. They are all objects to be negated.

100.

Worldly activities do not stop until death; we should try to search for a time within our daily lives to practice the Dharma. Now that we have met with such a profound system, in which the entire method for the achievement of enlightenment is accessible, it would be very sad if we did not try to make the Dharma have some impact on our lives.

101.

Those who wish to achieve omniscience should be single-pointed, attentive, and mentally humble, motivated by a wish to help other sentient beings, pay full attention with their minds, look at the spiritual masters with their eyes, and listen to the spiritual masters with their ears.

102.

Unless the mind of the teacher is tamed, there is no hope of the teacher taming others. Teachers should be restrained in their demeanor; their minds should be protected from distractions by the power of concentration. They should be equipped with the faculty of wisdom, penetrating the appearance of phenomena. If we possess higher training in ethical discipline, our minds are said to be tamed.

103.

Imagine a wide ocean with a golden yoke adrift upon it. In the depth of the ocean swims a single blind turtle, who surfaces for air once every hundred years. How rare would it be for the turtle to surface with its head through the hole in the yoke? The Buddha said that attaining a precious human rebirth is rarer than that.

104.

All the teachings associated with achievement of favorable rebirth in the future are said to belong to the category of small scope. Teachings related to the practice of achieving personal liberation are teachings of the middle scope. Practitioners of middle scope engage in the practice of this, concentration, and wisdom, and then eliminate the delusions and achieve liberation from suffering and rebirth. Teachings that outline the techniques for achieving omniscience of Buddhahood, both Sutric and Tantric, are teachings related to practitioners of great scope.

105.

We should train our minds so that our lives will not be wasted—not even for a month or a day—and prepare for the moment of death. When faced with death, the best practitioners will be delighted, the midlevel practitioners will be well prepared, and even the lowest practitioners will have no regret.

106.

Sufferings are a reality, and simply mentally avoiding them will not resolve the problem. We need to actually confront suffering, face it and analyze it, examine it, determine its causes, and find out how best to cope with it.

107.

A practitioner of the Dharma thinks daily about death and reflects upon the sufferings of human beings: the suffering at the time of birth, the suffering of aging, the suffering of sickness, and the suffering of death. Every day, Tantric practitioners go through the death process in their imagination.

108.

Half of our lives is spent in sleep; for ten years we are children and for twenty years we are old, and the time in between is tormented, so there is hardly any time for the practice of the Dharma.

109.

Karma is created by an agent, a person, a living being. Living beings are nothing other than the self, imputed on the basis of the continuity of consciousness. The nature of consciousness is luminosity and clarity. It is an agent of knowing that is preceded by an earlier moment of consciousness that is its cause.

110.

The Buddha is the master who shows us the path of enlightenment, the Dharma is the actual refuge in which we seek protection from suffering, and the Sangha consists of spiritual companions through the stages of the path.

111.

The degree of your commitment to serious practice depends very much upon how convinced you are, how deep your conviction is in the law of cause and effect, how fully you believe that undesirable sufferings and misfortunes are the consequences of negative actions, and how convinced you are that desirable consequences, like happiness, pleasure, and prosperity, are the results of positive actions.

112.

If the motivation is right, although the action itself might appear quite violent, it will bring about happiness, whereas if the motivation is wrong and devious, then even though the action might seem beneficial and positive, in reality, it will be negative action.

113.

When the body is weakened by certain diseases, you get angry, and when it is healthier, you have attachment. Birth is inevitably followed by death and death is followed by another rebirth. Thus, our body becomes the cause for the arising of delusions. It is only in nirvana that the delusions are totally dissolved in reality.

114.

There are two types of compassion. One type is just a wish that sentient beings be free from suffering. The other is more powerful: I shall take the responsibility for freeing sentient beings from suffering. Compassion and renunciation differ only in their object and objective. Renunciation is focused upon yourself; it is your wish that you be liberated from suffering. Compassion is directed toward other sentient beings; it is your wish that all beings be liberated from suffering.

115.

Patience is a state of mind that forbears in the face of harms inflicted by others. There are three types of patience. The first is not being upset by harms inflicted by others, the second is voluntarily taking suffering upon yourself, and the third is being able to endure the sufferings involved in the practice of the Dharma.

116.

We should think of our future, for life after death is something we know little about and our fate is unpredictable. If there is life after death, then it is very important to think about it and prepare for it.

117.

You have to achieve a profound realization of shunyata, or emptiness, the ultimate level of reality. This can be accomplished as a result of your practice and having encounters with your guru.

118.

When all your attachments disappear like the beggar with no possessions, you are then not entangled with all worldly concerns. Even in Tantric teachings, practitioners will not get attached to any sensual object that they use as a part of their practice.

119.

When practitioners gain experience of emptiness, the ultimate reality of all phenomena, a change comes about in their perception. It is different from that of ordinary people in the sense that it transcends the conventional way of viewing the world.

120.

At an experiential level, tukdam refers to a mystical state between life and death, wherein consciousness is withdrawn to the heart. It is at this point that practitioners' power of meditation actually preserves their bodies without decaying.

121.

The core of mind training is the cultivation and growth of Mahayana Buddhism's highest spiritual ideal, the generation of the awakening mind or bodhicitta. This refers to the altruistic aspiration to attain perfect enlightenment for the benefit of all beings.

122.

Our true enemy resides inside ourselves, not outside. We often get insulted and disappointed when others hurt or betray us. We are outraged when provoked for no reason, and at others' success, we experience pangs of jealousy. This is so because deep down we tend to cherish ourselves. Only the joyful mind can help you to feel good.

123.

We have enough religions. Enough religions but not enough real human beings. Religions should learn from each other, respect each other, and yet retain their identity. People have a right to choose their food from their spiritual basket.

124.

Violence can never create anything stable. This is like an eternal law. Only a wise, loving, patient intelligence can create anything that is durable. Altruism is the right source of happiness and contentment. Also, nonviolence is the only way of the oppressed people to develop a lasting peace.

125.

Even if we can recite the entire Tripitaka by heart but are egotistical and do harm to others, we are not practicing the Dharma. Dharma's practice makes us real, faithful, honest, and humble. We also need to help others, show them respect, and sacrifice ourselves for them.

126.

Renunciation is not just for people who possess passions and delusions. It is for all whose minds still contain even the slightest trace of illusions. Even the great arhats are unable to see the two truths, the relative and the absolute, simultaneously.

127.

Living in a monastery, wearing a monk's robe, and occupying yourself with advanced practices, pujas, mantra recitation, and prostrations seem to be Dharmic activities. However, if your mind is disturbed or distracted by minor external things of the world, all this amounts to nothing.

128.

Just as even the least irritation is a basis for aversion, so too can the smallest, seemingly natural desire change into obsessive and ever-increasing greed. Ignorance is a master that uses aversion to repel its enemies and desire and attachment to increase its potency.

129.

The realization of emptiness can only be attained by combining calm, one-pointed concentration and insight. Without this, living virtuously and reciting mantras and prayers, even though beneficial for us, will offer only temporary advantages. To attain perfect peace, the root of illusion has to be eradicated. Thus, the ultimate Dharma is the elimination of all illusion through the realization of emptiness.

130.

In order to realize the nonconceptual perception of profound emptiness, we must first familiarize ourselves with the idea, then develop an intellectual understanding of it. Once the emptiness of the object appears clearly in meditation, emptiness becomes a nonconceptual realization. The initial consciousness of emptiness depends on correct reasoning, which is the basis of wisdom.

131.

Physical illness or discomfort can be subdued by mental happiness. Mental satisfaction can subdue physical pain. On the other hand, if a person is mentally unhappy, with too much worry and stress, physical comfort cannot subdue that mental anxiety. The mental level is more important.

132.

Buddhist literature mentions that there is a limitation to any physical training because the physical level is grosser. With training, you can jump some remarkable distance or height, but there are still limits. But since the mind is formless, if you make it familiar with certain things, there are no limitations.

133.

Our mind is formless, shapeless, and although in one way it is very difficult to control, in another it is very easy to control: by transformation. Transformation at the mental level comes about entirely through voluntary willingness, through enthusiasm. No external force can change our mind.

134.

From the Buddhist viewpoint, everybody has Buddha-nature or *tathagatagarbha* or Buddha seed. As long as clear-light is there, the Buddha seed is there. Clear-light is the ultimate source, the ultimate cause of consciousness, so as long as consciousness is there, the ultimate source must be there. That, roughly speaking, is Buddha-nature. That is the potential to become all-knowing.

135.

We can achieve enlightenment only through the practice of meditation; without it there is no way we can transform our minds. By the process of training, habituation, cultivation, and cleansing your mind, you can actually transform your mind.

136.

To achieve enlightenment, there are two practices: Sutra and Tantra. The purpose of Tantra is to provide a faster path so that qualified students can be of service to others quite quickly. Here students exercise their imaginations in a practice called *deity yoga*.

137.

If you have received a Tantric empowerment and you meditate as explained in the tantras, you visualize your body as the body of a deity and meditate on that. When you enter into the practice of highest yoga tantra, you focus not simply on the whole body but on specific points within the body. You focus on the energies flowing through the channels in the body and also on a particular drop within the channels.

138.

A combination of wisdom and compassionate motivation is to be kept in mind in deity yoga. Thus a single consciousness realizes emptiness and also appears compassionately in the form of an altruistic deity. Thus, a combination of wisdom and compassionate motivation in our consciousness is imperative for progress in the practice of Tantra.

139.

You can meditate simply on the nature of the mind, the clarity and mere luminosity of the mind. You have to stop thinking about your past and future experiences and plans. Once you stop the arising of conceptual thoughts, the mind will be free to identify its mere luminous nature.

140.

Since we are social animals, we are a part of a society, and in order to live happily in that society, it is essential to have community spirit and fully cooperate with each other. In order to achieve genuine cooperation, friendship is the key factor, and trust is the basis of friendship—not money, power, education, or intelligence. If there is real trust, friendship comes naturally.

THE THREE PRINCIPAL
ASPECTS OF THE PATH

His Holiness the Dalai Lama

Master Nagarjuna's "The Fundamental Wisdom of the Middle Way" says, "To you, who out of great compassion expounded the sublime truth in order to eliminate all views, to you, Gautama Buddha, I pay homage" (1967).

This verse comes from the twenty-seventh chapter of Master Nagarjuna's text. At the end of that book, Master Nagarjuna pays his homage in gratitude to the Buddha for his teaching. Dependent origination and the fundamental treaties of the middle way are explanations of the essence of the Buddha's teaching, which is the perfection of the wisdom sutras, and so, the meaning of this particular verse is that the Buddha showed us the path to free ourselves from suffering. Out of his compassion for us, he gave his holy teaching; that the suffering we undergo happens because of conditions, and ultimately the condition or the cause of suffering is ignorance. Owing to ignorance, it is very clear to us that we suffer because we all don't want suffering, but we want happiness; although happiness is what we want and suffering is what we don't want, we constantly suffer, and therefore we have all kinds of problems in our lives. Of all the seven billion people on this earth, nobody wants any suffering but only happiness, but why suffering happens to us is because of our ignorance. In Buddhism, pain and pleasure come from their causes and conditions, and suffering ultimately comes from ignorance, and within ignorance, there is a mere not knowing about things. Another type of ignorance is the distorted kind of ignorance (view), misconceptions about reality—reality in the sense of how things come about through causes and conditions and also the ultimate reality of how things exist, *suchness* as it is called. And therefore, one has to eliminate the ignorance that is within us, ignorance about the law of causality and also ignorance about the dependent nature of things. The Buddha has shown us means to overcome them, and they can't go away merely by praying or wishing for them to go away, or by doing some kind of prostration, and making offerings, and worshipping the three jewels, and so forth. What must happen within us is the overcoming of ignorance by knowing the reality of how things come about through cause and condition, as well as how things are, ultimately their nature, and therefore, that's what we must cultivate and develop: the wisdom of realizing the nature of things. Hence, you can see that Master Nagarjuna pays his homage to the Buddha where he says "enthused by your great compassion you expound sublime truth in order to eliminate all views."

Now here, when he uses the term *view*, it should be clear to us that this view is not the right kind of view about causality or about the dependent nature of things, but all kinds of distorted views. In this context you need to generate this wisdom. By cultivating the right view, we have to overcome ignorance, and therefore Buddhism teaches about the dependent nature of things, how things come about interdependently and within it; as I said earlier, there is the law of causality as well as how things are interrelated, interconnected, and therefore we have to develop the wisdom of knowing the causality of things as well as their final reality. Through this wisdom, we can overcome our ignorance and thereby the suffering. Thus, Master Nagarjuna pays his homage by saying, "To you, Gautama Buddha, I pay homage."

In dependent origination, there is no ceasing, no arising,
no annihilation, no permanence,

No coming, no going, no separateness, and no sameness.

I prostrate to the consummate Buddha,

The supreme among all teachers, the one who taught this
peace, which is freed of elaborations.

The Buddha does not wash away negativities with water;

Nor does he clear away suffering with his hands;

Nor can he transfer his own qualities to us;

He shows the true path; by that alone are beings liberated.

—The Buddha,
quoted from *Udanavargavivarna*

These verses contain the words of the Buddha. They show us how we go about the practice of Buddhism and how the system works. Buddha doesn't wash away any of the negativities with water, nor does he clear away suffering with his hands. Buddha can't take away our sins and negative actions with his hands, nor can he transfer his own qualities to us—quality, in the sense of Buddha's realization of how things are and also his having overcome all the negativities within his own mind and having seen all things exactly as they are. So these can't be transported into other sentient beings. Buddha himself became a Buddha not merely through the blessings of the past Buddhas, but also Buddha became enlightened by working toward enlightenment in such a way that he put in effort lifetime after lifetime until he reached the stage of Buddhahood. During those lifetimes of working to become Buddha, he worked to overcome all the defilements and then also actualized the basic clear-light of the luminous nature of the mind that we also have, and therefore, it shows that the Buddha was not an enlightened being right from the beginning. He was first of all an ordinary being like us. Then by applying the teachings that he had received within himself, and by applying those teachings and overcoming the negativities, and as well as actualizing this clear-light or the luminous nature of mind that we also have, he finally became somebody who is an all-knowing one, an enlightened being, the Buddha. Therefore, what it shows is that we also need to put effort into practicing the teaching of the Buddha. So, the way Buddha helps us is only by teaching the paths as it says at the end of the second verse: "He shows the true paths, and by that alone are beings liberated." Thus, by showing how the nature of things is, the reality of things, just as Buddha himself has learned and just as he also became fully aware through his own experience, he has shown the path to enlightenment, Buddhahood. Therefore, the way to overcome suffering in Buddhism is not only through prayers, but also by developing and cultivating the wisdom, knowing the reality of things, and therefore knowing that wisdom overcomes and eliminates the ignorance that is the root of the suffering. So, in this way, we also have to take the path Buddha has shown.

These two verses basically show the kind of right view we should develop in order to overcome the wrong kinds of view that we have. Wrong views are in terms of the four aspects of seeing unclean phenomenon, like our body, which is impure and unclean, as pure and clean; seeing things that are impermanent as permanent and unchanging; seeing things that are in the nature of suffering as being pleasant; and then where things are selfless, perceiving and conceiving the things have self or self-nature. Therefore, in order to overcome these four kinds of wrong views or misconceptions, what we need to develop are the opposite: to see the unclean—things like the body—as unclean, to see impermanent things as impermanent, to see the suffering nature of things as being in that nature, and also to see that things have no independent existence or selfhood. Therefore, why do we have these perceptions—the perception of things as being clean and permanent, whereas they are unclean and impermanent? Why this happens is because we see the cleanliness or the permanence in things as having some kind of objective existence. If we give careful thought to our body, it is in its very nature to be impermanent and changing, but when we are not giving it due thought but are taking it for granted, then when we perceive ourselves in the usual way, we see ourselves as clean, permanent, pleasant, and having a self-nature. If we think carefully, we will see the unclean nature, suffering nature, impermanent nature, and non-self-nature of things. We have this conception of things as being clean and so forth, because of the ignorance that is not able to realize or see the disparity between how things appear and what the reality is. Therefore, what we have to see is that things arise through causes and conditions.

As things arise through causes and conditions, what we can see is that something arises or is produced if the right conditions are complete. That thing will not arise or happen if the conditions are lacking, so when unfavorable conditions are met, things cease to exist or they go away, and when favorable conditions are met, things arise, and that's how things happen in the world and actually happen in our lives. Therefore, in this first verse, with regard to the nature of things, Master Nagarjuna refs to the process of ceasing and arising, and then in regard to the continuity of things, he mentions that things that come through dependent arising have no annihilation and no permanence. From the point of view of the object, he touches on the points of no coming and no going, and then from the point of view of terminology or in terms of pairs of things, he refers to the things that come about through dependence as having no separateness and no sameness. So, in this verse, what Master Nagarjuna actually is trying to show is that to us, things usually seem to have some kind of objective existence. That they appear to have some objective, independent existence, and that we must not be satisfied with the mere appearance of the things but make an analysis of how things actually exist. When we analyze the nature of things, what we see is that we don't find either the arising or ceasing.

Similarly, when we look at things as permanent, then in the ultimate nature of things, there is no permanence and no annihilation. Here Nagarjuna is not saying that things do not arise, or that they are not produced and that they don't cease, and so forth. Of course, these processes exist: things do arise through causes and conditions, through dependence and on other factors; and they do cease through dependence on causes and conditions; and then there are also things that are permanent—the true cessation of things as well as coming and going and one in many. These things are there, but what Master Nagarjuna basically is showing here is that when we do analysis into the real nature of things, then we don't find any certitude. Nothing can be found through this ultimate analysis. So within that perception, there is no coming, no going, no arising, no cessation. So he is not saying that things have no coming, no going. In conventional terms, which we all know, things do come and go, but the reason that Master Nagarjuna says that things that are in the nature of dependence don't have cessation is because they do not have any objective existence. In that sense of arising, they are dependently arisen, and the reasoning he uses is dependence, because things are designated through dependence, and therefore they don't have any independent essence or objective existence of their own. The main reason that he is using to prove that things have no coming and no going is in the ultimate sense, and he is not saying that things do not have coming and going in conventional terms.

What these two verses of Master Nagarjuna show is the dependent origination of things in the sense of how things are dependent upon designation by mind. Once you understand this well—how things are dependent and designated—then you will also see how things are related to each other, how things are relative as well. That, in turn, will lead you to the insight of how things are causally brought about, that causes and conditions brought about their effects. The law of causality will be understood better, and therefore these verses seem to show the subtle understanding or level of dependent origination. Once you understand the subtle nature of how things are dependently originated, designated dependently, then it will be easier; you will be able to understand the relativity of things or the causality of things very easily, and therefore that is how you will develop your insight into the law of causality, how things are relative. In order to gain that deeper understanding into the subtle dependent designation of things, what you would use is the reasoning of how things are brought about through causes and conditions as well. Therefore, when you see that things are brought about through causes and conditions, you will be led into the insight of how they are related, and therefore into the subtle dependent designation–related nature of things. You will be able to see the compatibility between how things are empty by nature, empty of independent existence, and the how things are dependently originated. So you will be able to see that what is dependent origination is empty and what is empty is also dependent.

Even in modern physics, particularly quantum physics, the scientists talk about how things have no objective existence. So, this concept is very similar to the Buddhist idea or understanding of the dependently related nature of things.

The reason why I am giving this teaching and also explaining these things that I have done before is in order for you to know what Buddhism actually means. So many people, of course, or many of you here, might consider yourselves Buddhist, but then what we see is that you are fond of reciting mantras and prayers. Of course, reciting mantras is also there in other traditions: in Hinduism and Islam, and then also we see Christian practitioners saying different hymns and mantras and prayers. With regard to the practice of religion, people follow all these different traditions, and also there is the practice of tolerance, not harming others, and self-contentment, self-discipline, and so forth.

So in terms of practice, recitation of mantras and prayers, all the religious traditions have these practices and these are common to all. When it comes to real religion or spiritual traditions and practice, it's not only about prayers or worshipping the gods. People of course say prayers in front of statues, and these are common to different religions, but then we as Buddhists must understand the difference between the religious traditions as well. The difference lies in the philosophical understanding, or the philosophical view, of these various religious traditions. Within the world religions, there are basically two kinds: theistic religious groups and the nontheistic religions. Within the nontheistic religions there are differences. For example, within the nontheistic religious traditions, there are those religions that assert some kind of independent or personal self that is permanent, single, and autonomous, but the difference between these other world religious traditions and Buddhism is the understanding or the view of the dependent origination of things. So if you are a Buddhist, what you must understand is this unique feature or unique characteristic of Buddhism, which is dependent origination, and I have always been telling everyone, especially Buddhists, that they must become 21st-century Buddhists. When people usually say they are Buddhist, they think in terms of who their parents are and what religion they follow. Accordingly, you may say that you are Buddhist or you belong to this or that religion because of your parents, but that must not be our reason. We must not be carried away by blind faith but must understand the broad framework of Buddhism and the teachings of the Buddha, and for that, we must use reasoning so that we draw our inspiration and faith based on reason. That type of person with sharp faculties and those who use reason to bring about faith in their religion become authentic 21st-century Buddhists in the sense of developing reason based on the teaching of the Buddha. So, what we must try to develop is reason-based faith in the teaching of the Buddha and not just follow Buddhism as a custom saying that your parents are Buddhist and therefore you are Buddhist and so forth.

Even some scientists today go to the length of saying they do believe in rebirth, which is also talked about in Buddhism. As Buddhists, we must be able to understand this unique feature of the teaching of the Buddha. Hence the reason why I gave this introductory talk is in order for you to understand this. Of course I am not trying to boss over you, or claim that I know so much about Buddhism and all that, but I merely wish that you could become Buddhist based on your understanding of the teaching of the Buddha through reason. When I visited some Himalayan regions and interacted with people, once I asked some people about the religion they follow. They said they were Buddhist and when I asked what Buddhism is, they replied to me that Buddhism is about taking refuge in the Buddha, Dharma, and Sangha. I asked them further what is a Buddha? Who is a Buddha? There was no answer and then I still asked again whether the Buddha, Brahma, and Ishwar and so forth are the same or not. These people answered that they are the same, which shows their ignorance about the teaching of the Buddha and what the Buddha is and how someone becomes a Buddha. And so, this must not be our case.

We must try to develop understanding of Buddhism, and therefore the Buddha himself has said, "Oh Bhikshus and the Wise. Just as gold is tested through burning, cutting and rubbing, likewise by examining my words thoroughly, and only then, accept them, not merely out of respect for me." So, we must follow what the Buddha has said. By using logic and reason, we must draw conclusions about the teaching of the Buddha and when we use logic, what we must try to find out is whether the teachings of the Buddha contradict reality or reason. If the teachings of the Buddha contradict reason and experiment, we must not take them literally. Of course, in many religions of the world, what is mentioned is that you must simply follow the founder teachers, whereas in Buddha's case it's different. He has given us this freedom to check his own teaching, examine his own teaching, but of course I am not saying that Buddhism is the best religion! I never say that and whether some religion is best for somebody or not depends on the individual case, as that particular religion and teaching may be most suited and most beneficial for that person. If a particular religion is most beneficial to someone, then that could be considered the best religion for that person and we cannot generalize or say that this or that religion is best. We have to check individually, and therefore what we must always use is reason and logic in line with the teaching of the Buddha, and what is important is to see whether the teachings of Buddha are consonant with reason or not.

In the Indian philosophical traditions, there are so many texts that are written on logic, whether they are Buddhist texts or non-Buddhist texts; there are so many of them that use logic because of the importance of reason. And, for example, within the Buddhist Mahayana tradition, we have masters like Dignaga, Dharmakirti, Shantarakshita, and Kamalashila who have written all these great texts on Pramana, logic and epistemology. And there are many translations of the texts of these masters, such as the Master Dignaga's *Pramana Samuccaya*, and then other texts on logic and epistemology— Master Dharmakirti's seven texts on logic and epistemology, and Master Shantarakshita's text on logic and epistemology called *Tattvasangraha*, and his disciple Kamalashila's commentary on the difficult points of a particular text by Shantarakshita. What this shows is that the path the Tibetan masters have taken reveals a keen interest in learning and using reason and logic. So if you know this system of logic and how logic is used, it can help you to make a critical analysis and develop sharp intelligence. It's quite something that the complete texts of these masters have been translated into Tibetan only and not into other Buddhist languages like Chinese and so forth. But in Tibetan, we have all these texts on logic and epistemology written by these masters and these should be considered our treasure. Thus, we can read them in our own language and therefore we must pay attention and take interest in studying these texts on logic.

I usually tell people everywhere that the Tibetan Buddhist tradition is an authentic Nalanda tradition deriving from Nalanda Monastic University, and you will find it to be true if you read the texts that we have in translation in the Tengyur and Kangyur canonical literature.

If you read them carefully and understand them, you will understand how Tibetan Buddhism is the authentic Nalanda tradition.

In the 8th century, at the invitation of the Tibetan king Trisong Detsen, two great Indian masters brought this Nalanda tradition to Tibet—Master Shantarakshita, whom we refer to as Khenchen Shiwatso (the great abbot), and also the precious Guru Padmasambhava. These two great masters of India were invited to Tibet. We usually refer to the three of them as the Trio Khen-lob-choe-sum, where *Khen* refers to Shantarakshita, *lob* means Master Padmasambhava, and *choe* for the religious King Trisong Detsen. So, in order to establish this authentic Nalanda tradition in Tibet, Master Shantarakshita took the main responsibility of teaching Buddhism to the Tibetans and establishing the monastic tradition, and he also looked after and supervised the translation of the texts as well. In order for him to be able to carry out this work in Tibet, he had the help of the able Padmasambhava, who was mainly responsible for overcoming the obstacles to the establishment of Buddhism in Tibet—obstacles from humans and nonhumans, or spirits. Without Padmasambhava's help with the translation of texts into Tibetan and in overcoming these evil spirits and humans who were against the establishment of Buddhism, the master Shantarakshita would not have been able to carry out his work of teaching and establishing the monastic ordination and system. So, thanks to those two great masters, who themselves were from the Nalanda monastic institution, Buddhism was established in Tibet. Therefore, for these reasons, we can call Tibetan Buddhism the authentic tradition of Nalanda. With these three masters, we have the early establishment of the Nyingma tradition in Tibet, and then later on, other Buddhist traditions, such as Sakya and Kagyu, and then the Kadam tradition as well as the Ganden or Geluk tradition, which also evolved in Tibet. If you look at the history, the Indian masters, who actually became the main teachers of these Tibetan masters who established these traditions, were from Nalanda, and therefore all these Tibetan Buddhist traditions follow the authentic Nalanda tradition. Within the Tibetan Buddhist tradition, after the coming of Master Atisha to Tibet in the 11th century, the Kadam tradition was established and Master Atisha himself wrote the text called *The Lamp for the Path to Enlightenment*, which later became the basis for what is known as the Lamrim tradition in Tibet. If you look at the different Tibetan Buddhist traditions, we have texts that follow the Lamrim tradition established by different masters. For example, in the text written in the Nyingma tradition, we have what we call the *Trilogy of Ease and Comfort* (the actual name is *Finding Rest in the Nature of Mind: Trilogy of Rest*), and in the Kagyu tradition, we have the text called *The Jewel Ornament of Liberation* by Gampopa, and then in the Sakya tradition, we have the text that deals with the three visions. All these texts follow the Lamrim tradition whose layout is established by Master Atisha. Later on in the 14th century, Master Tsongkhapa came to Tibet and established the Geluk tradition. He wrote different texts on the stages of the path, Lamrim, following the basic text by Master Atisha, as well as the different commentaries by Kadampa masters. And the essence of all these texts he wrote is what we are going to look at in the "The Three Principal Aspects of the Path," which was in fact written in the form of a letter to one his disciples.

THE THREE PRINCIPAL ASPECTS
OF THE PATH

I bow down to the venerable Gurus.

I will explain as well as I am able
The essence of all the teachings of the Conqueror,
The path praised by the Conqueror's children,
The entrance for the fortunate who desire liberation.

Listen with a clear mind, you fortunate ones
Who are not attached to the joys of cyclic existence,
Who strive to make good use of leisure and opportunity,
And direct your mind to the path pleasing to the Buddha
Without pure determination to be free, there is no way to end
The craving for existence that binds beings.
Thus, from the outset seek renunciation.
Reverse attraction to this life,

By reflecting on how leisure and opportunity are difficult
to find: and how life is ephemeral and without span.
Reverse attraction to future lives,
By repeatedly thinking of the infallibility
of karma and its effects, and the misery of Samsara.

Contemplating thus, when you do not for an instant
Admire the splendors of cyclic existence,
And remain intent on liberation day and night
Renunciation is then born in you.

Renunciation, however, if not tempered by
a pure mind of enlightenment,
Does not bring forth the perfect bliss of
unsurpassed enlightenment.
Therefore, the wise ones generate the excellent mind
of enlightenment

Swept by the current of the four powerful rivers;
Tied by strong bonds of karma, so hard to undo;
Caught in the iron net of self-grasping;
Completely enveloped by the darkness of ignorance;

Born and reborn in boundless cyclic existence;
Ceaselessly tormented by the three miseries;
Thinking of your mothers in this condition,
Generate the supreme mind (of enlightenment).

Although you train in renunciation and
the mind of enlightenment,
Without wisdom which realizes the ultimate reality,
You cannot cut the root of cyclic existence.
Therefore, strive to understand dependent arising.

One who sees the infallible cause and effect
Of all phenomena in cyclic existence and peace,
And destroys all focuses of apprehension,
Has entered into the path which pleases the Buddha.

Appearances are infallible dependent arising;
And emptiness is the understanding that is free of assertions.
As long as these two are seen as distinct,
You have not yet realized the intent of the Buddha.

When these two realizations are simultaneous,
Where the mere sight of infallible dependent origination
Concurrently destroys all modes of grasping
through definite discernment,
At that time the analysis of the (profound) view is perfected.

Furthermore, appearances refute the extreme of existence;
Emptiness refutes the extreme of nonexistence;
When you understand that emptiness arises
in the form of cause and effect,
You are not captivated by the view of extremes.

Oh! Child, once you have realized the points
Of the Three Principles of the Path,
Seek solitude and cultivate strong determination
And quickly reach the final goal!

—Lama Tsongkhapa

Regarding the Three Principal Aspects of the Path, how the teaching is dealt with in this text and in the Lamrim texts is different. Here in the stages of the path texts, the Lamrim is written for the benefit of three types of beings. So, the approach is to benefit these three types of beings or three types of individuals—those with small, medium, and superior capacities. In accordance with the needs of these three types of beings, the Lam-rim text has been laid out. In our text, the approach is slightly different. And in *Ratnavali*, which translates as *The Jewel Garland*, Master Nagarjuna says the teaching of the Buddha basically is to attain the means to higher rebirth, and then ultimately the means for what is known as definite goodness, or liberation, and finally enlightenment.

So, the Three Principal Aspects of the Path are mainly focusing on these points of how we should escape this samsara and reach the omniscient stage and attain the state of liberation. Of course when we talk about liberation, we should talk and base our liberation on freedom from samsara and all defilements and the trainings that lead to that. With regard to the practice of morality, what the basis of morality basically constitutes is the practice of restraint from harming others. Therefore, when we talk about morality, we must think of not harming others and keeping that percept of not harming others. That comes along within the practice of developing the path to liberation, and the main path, or the means to reach that highest liberation, is of course the practice of bodhicitta in order to reach the all-knowing state of Buddhahood. Bodhicitta is rooted in love and compassion (or loving kindness and compassion), and when we develop bodhicitta, we should first develop compassion as well. Compassion here is the main thing that we generate in developing bodhicitta. Now compassion is this attitude or this wish for others to be free from suffering, and when you wish to develop this attitude of wishing others to be free from suffering, what is really important is for you to actually understand and be aware of what suffering actually is.

If you don't know what suffering means, then you cannot have this real, genuine wish for others to be free from suffering. Hence, we have to know the suffering that is within ourselves and we have to actually acknowledge and become aware of the condition that we ourselves are in. We are in the condition called the condition of suffering and therefore by becoming aware of our own suffering, it will be much more effective for us to develop compassion toward others. Therefore you have to develop this wish to be free from suffering for yourself first, and that is what is known as the *thought of definite emergence*, usually translated as *renunciation*. Now, when you wish to develop this renunciation for samsara, this cycle of existence, you must be aware of suffering and wish to be free of this suffering. And within this process, what we have is where we are going to lead ourselves—toward liberation; that is, by practicing, applying, and cultivating the three higher trainings of morality, concentration, and wisdom, we lead ourselves to liberation. What we actually develop is this deep insight into the real nature of the mind itself. Seeing the nature of the mind itself actually helps us to abandon the illusions that are within us and experience the suchness of the mind. We are here not only looking for mere liberation from this conditioned existential suffering of samsara. And we are not looking for mere freedom from karma and the afflictive emotions that are the causes of suffering, but we are also looking to develop the bodhicitta. We aim toward being fully enlightened, or attaining Buddhahood, not just nirvana, where we have only overcome the delusions that are within our mind. In these defilements, such as the three poisons of ignorance, attachment, and hatred, we are also looking into overcoming even the subtle residues or stains of these defilements that are within our minds. Which means we are trying to attain what is known as Samyaksambodhi, Buddhahood: this total freedom from all defilements in the mind. In order to reach enlightenment or Buddhahood, what we must develop is, first of all, this thought of renunciation, wishing to be free from samsara, and then also develop loving compassion, which in turn leads to the experience of bodhicitta, this altruistic state of mind, and thus we reach Buddhahood for the benefit of all the sentient beings.

Now it is not enough to develop these two principles of renunciation and bodhicitta; these must in turn be complemented or helped by the wisdom of realizing the real nature of things, which means how things are dependently designated, and therefore how they are empty of independent existence. Using this wisdom of realizing things to be dependently originated, dependently designated, we should be better able to develop this wish to be out of suffering and also develop bodhicitta. Wisdom is the critical realization that is very essential in the practice of the path. It is very important to gain insight into the empty nature of things, and so in this way, this understanding will lead you to overcome the defilements that are within the mind. When you develop this wisdom and see reality as it is without any kind of cognitive error in your mind, then what happens is that these defilements themselves dissolve into the very nature of mind itself, which is to say you reach what is called cessation and you develop renunciation and bodhicitta. Then these are embraced by correct views. And within views, we have the view, in Buddhism, of what is also known as the four seals of the Buddha's teaching, which says that all composite things are impermanent, everything is in the nature of suffering and defilement, everything is without self, and finally that nirvana is peace. The view that we are talking about here is mainly deep understanding into how things are empty of an independent way of existing.

Now, I will explain the text itself on the Three Principal Aspects of the Path.

The homage to venerable gurus and the first verse after that show the pledge to compose the text, and the second verse is urging us to bow down to the venerable gurus. I will explain the first verse.

Master Tsongkhapa urges disciples who are receptive to listen to the teachings; "Listen with a clear mind, you fortunate ones who are not attached to the joys of cyclic existence, who strive to make good use of leisure and opportunity, and direct your mind to the path pleasing to the Buddha." And in the next verse he says, "Without pure determination to be free, there is no way to end the craving for existence that binds beings, thus, from the outset seek renunciation, reverse attraction to this life." This first verse shows the reason why we must cultivate renunciation. Within this context, of course, when we talk about this thought, cultivating renunciation, or the thought of renouncing samsara, we must think about the suffering nature of samsara. Within suffering, there are three kinds of suffering. The first is known as the suffering of pain, or the painful experiences that are obvious to us as beings as suffering and misery. There is also the second type of suffering, which is known as the suffering of change. These two are not the main focus in thinking of renunciation from samsara. We are not thinking only of overcoming these two types of suffering, because in the first type of suffering, the *suffering of pain*, even animals are aware of it as something unwanted; regarding the second type of suffering—the *suffering of change*—even those who do not belong to Buddhist traditions, as such, are aware of this kind of suffering as being unwanted. Therefore we must understand overcoming suffering within the context of the teachings of Buddha. This is the third type of suffering, the deeper type of suffering, which is called the *existential all-pervasive and conditioned suffering*. This kind of suffering happens under the influence of our negative thoughts and afflictive emotions, the delusions. So long as a birth is under the influence of these delusions, that kind of birth will be suffering. This very existence itself is termed as existential all-pervasive and conditioned suffering; so this is what we actually target when we think about developing and cultivating renunciation. Having given thought to this kind of deeper suffering of cyclic existence itself, which is brought about by delusion, when you are pursuing that path or total freedom from this kind of suffering, then you actually develop the authentic aspiration of renunciation. When you aspire to reach this goal, then you have developed a genuine sense of renunciation as well. This is what Buddhism means by renunciation. That we must overcome the attraction to future lives. In order to be able to do that, we must focus on or think about the infallibility of the law of karma and also the suffering nature of samsara, the cycle of existence. When we talk about this karma, karma means action. We talk about the effects of actions. What we also come to understand is that actions bring about pain and pleasure, which happen when there are beings that are able to experience sensation or feelings. On the basis of these experiences, we talk about pain and pleasure being brought about through karma. Here it is very clearly mentioned in Master Shantideva's *Guide to the Bodhisattva Way of Life*, where he mentions the point of how a certain flower, like a lotus, has its shape, color, fragrance, and so forth. So, here it says these are due to their own causes and conditions, and the shape and color and smell or fragrance of the lotus are due to their different conditions. He goes further to point out that though these are due to their respective causes and conditions, when it comes to beginningless pain and suffering and pleasure, they come about through their own causes and conditions or karma. Now here, of course, we can talk about the pain and pleasure in terms of how they are related to certain experiences that beings actually feel and undergo. We can talk about the environment, and our karma having some effect on the environment, and therefore, we can go through certain experiences based on such karmas that are driven or mature in the form of environment. But basically, of course, there is some connection between our experience of pain and pleasure as beings and the environment; generally speaking, Master Shantideva says that the color, shape, and fragrance of a lotus are due to different causes and conditions that are preceding the lotus in the form of karmic imprints. When he was further asked where those causes and conditions come from, he responded by saying that they also come from their own causes and conditions. In this way, this is talking about the law of causality, which is very similar to Darwin's theory of evolution, which states that the things come from their causes and conditions that precede them. In the external world, of course, we have phenomena that come from causes and conditions, and internally, within the sentient beings, our body, for example, has its own causes and conditions that are material, and therefore these phenomena are within us or our own body. If you trace where they come from, you will find that they come from causes and conditions that have preceded them, and here we are talking about the material continuity of phenomena. In terms of their own continuity of things, they have their own continuity from the previous moments of the body. We can go back to the Big Bang, for example, and therefore the material continuity of the body that we have and the eternal environment have come from the Big Bang, and from even before that, perhaps. So because of this, Master Aryadeva has said in his text, *Four Hundred Verses*, that things have no beginning, as such. We cannot pinpoint the beginning of a phase, but there is an end to phenomena, and so when we look at the material world, we can see that the different things are brought about by their own causes and conditions, which have a similarity to them and which have concurrence to them or are conducive to certain effects. Similarly, this is the case with consciousness or the mind that we have. For example, if you think about the visual consciousness, how a visual consciousness is produced in order to look at something physical, something that has form and shape and all that, what happens is that the object form serves as a focal point. The material consciousness is there, and also within our eyes, or within the eye organ, there is the faculty that is known as the visual faculty, and so that faculty serves as what is known as the empowering condition, which brings about the visual consciousness. However, even with these two factors (the object and the visual faculty), it is not certain that a certain visual consciousness will arise. Therefore, what is needed is the actual consciousness that arises in the form of a visual consciousness, and hence, the visual consciousness must have a preceding moment of consciousness that serves as its substantial cause, and therefore what we have to understand is that the mere nature of the mind being clear and knowing can bring about substantial effects in the visual consciousness, which has the same characteristics or same features of clarity and cognitive, or knowing, nature.

Apart from something that has these qualities of knowing and clarity, matter itself cannot be a substantial cause of consciousness, even at the time of conception. If you think along these lines—that the consciousness is brought about by a substantial cause that is also in the nature of knowing and clarity—and therefore, if you were to look for the beginning of such a thing—it will be very difficult to find a beginning of consciousness. When somebody considers this more, of course the embryo in the body does start there at conception, but there should also be consciousness, which is conceived in the mother's womb, which allows the embryo to grow as a fetus and then become a child. Master Dharmakirti says that something that is not consciousness cannot be a substantial cause of consciousness; so what this really means is that the consciousness must be brought about by a substantial cause, which is also a consciousness and which has this nature of clarity and knowing. With that consciousness, what happens is we also have motivation in us. That motivation, which is a mental process with which we create mental karma or action, is that which in turn causes physical as well as verbal actions to arise.

The point I wish to make here is that karma, or action, has to have a certain motivation, which is what actually brings about or creates the result. Apart from karma, of course, the law of causality is something universal for all kinds of phenomena that are brought about by causes and conditions. When it comes to talking about karma bringing pain and pleasure, it has to do with the result of a certain motivation, a specific experience of beings, which creates that karma. The text says reverse your mind from samsara and cultivate the thought of renunciation. Now, in the actual practice of cultivating renunciation, it will be very effective if you can use what is said in the verse where it says, "Swept by the current of the four powerful rivers, tied by strong bonds of karma, so hard to undo, caught in the iron net of self-grasping, completely enveloped by the darkness of ignorance, born and reborn in boundless cyclic existence, ceaselessly tormented by the three miseries . . . generate the supreme mind (of enlightenment)." In the context of generating or cultivating the thought of renunciation, what you have to reverse is thinking about yourself alone. Focusing on your own condition is generating the thought of renunciation, so here we can now switch these lines for renunciation and apply them to the meditation on the bodhicitta accordingly. Here the four powerful rivers could refer to those of birth, aging, sickness, and death. When you are a child, bound by the strong bond of karma, this is a difficult restriction.

With regard to the next line, the one that mentions self-grasping, here self-grasping can be understood as the self-grasping at the existence of a real person. First you need to understand the very gross level of self-grasping, selflessness of a person, and then go into more subtle levels of understanding the self. The next line referring to the darkness of ignorance could be understood in terms of the ignorance that grasps the self of phenomenon (inherent existence) and so you should overcome this by understanding the emptiness of phenomenon. What happens to us is that because of our strong self-grasping to the independent existence of an individual self, we perceive beautiful things, and bad and good things, but due to our grasping at considering something as really bad and focusing on that further and further, more and more what happens is that this clinging to the badness in things or the goodness in things increases an exaggeration of things as being good, bad, or attractive or ugly. Owing to that, we create karma. Through karma, we bind ourselves to samsara and we are born again and again in this boundless ocean of existence, and therefore we ceaselessly are tormented by these three types of suffering: the suffering of pain, changeable suffering, and all-pervasive conditioned suffering. Now having used this verse this way to cultivate renunciation first, you then think about the suffering of yourself and the suffering nature of samsara from beginningless time.

You try to develop this thought of renunciation, wishing to be free from samsara, and then that same wish to be free of suffering should be directed toward others. Turn it toward others, and then you develop compassion, the wish for others to be out of suffering. So in this way, when you think about the wish to free yourself from suffering and get out of it, you generate or cultivate renunciation. When you turn your mind toward others and wish them to be free from suffering, then you actually cultivate compassion, and in this way, you can also generate renunciation. Think about the suffering nature of yourself and then on this verse: "Contemplating thus, when you do not for an instant admire the splendors of cyclic existence and remain intent on liberation day and night, renunciation is then born in you." This shows that having measured the concrete advantages of your renunciation, this thought to be free from samsara always persists. Here, when we think about the suffering nature of ourselves and others, and when we talk about it, what happens is that usually when we look in the world, we see that what people are actually attracted toward or run after is sensory pleasure and they try to draw satisfaction from that. The more we try to draw satisfaction based on sensory experiences alone, the more we get into trouble, and therefore, even though we are born as human beings, which is considered a higher rebirth, physically we are human beings but not evolved beings; because of so much obsession with sensory pleasures, we are almost like animals.

Mentally we could consider ourselves as animals, and that's what we don't want. What we have to also see is how, in the world, there are the painful experiences that we consider suffering, and also those experiences that we consider as being pleasant and pleasurable even though they are very changeable (these pleasures change into suffering), and because of our sensual pleasures, we are not able to see them to be in the nature of suffering. We are actually deceived by these appearances of apparent pleasure and pleasant things and experiences. Therefore, we suffer more and more, and hence we should see the senselessness of this kind of clinging and obsession with sensual pleasures and try to develop true happiness within ourselves. The root of suffering, which is ignorance, must be understood, ignorance sees reality in a distorted manner, and therefore, we must try to overcome it by developing the wisdom that sees the selfless nature of things, and then, in order to develop this, having understood the selfless nature of things, we should combine Shamatha and Vipashyana. For that, we have to, of course, develop single-pointed concentration in order to be able to combine wisdom and understanding with concentration so that we have a combined experience of Shamatha and Vipashyana, calm abiding and insight. And then in order to develop single-pointedness further, we base ourselves on moral principles and avoid negative actions. This is the way we should help ourselves to escape the suffering of samsara.

"Renunciation, however, if not tempered by a pure mind of enlightenment, does not bring forth the perfect bliss of unsurpassed enlightenment. Therefore, the wise ones generate the excellent mind of enlightenment," shows the reason why we must cultivate bodhicitta, this altruistic intention to become Buddha for the benefit of sentient beings. Now in order to cultivate bodhicitta within ourselves, the teaching also shows how we actually go about this cultivation, so the next verse is "Swept by the current of the four powerful rivers," which we spoke of earlier. This whole verse, which deals with generating the supreme mind of enlightenment, says, "Swept by the current of four powerful rivers, tied by strong bond of karma, so hard to undo, caught in the iron net of self-grasping; completely enveloped by the darkness of ignorance; born and reborn in boundless cyclic existence; ceaselessly tormented by the three miseries; thinking of your mothers in this condition, generate the supreme mind (of enlightenment)." This shows how we go about the cultivation of bodhicitta and then the measure of having completed our cultivation or development of bodhicitta. When you have genuine bodhicitta, this has to be understood using the same logic that is used for renunciation as well. In the practice of cultivating the path to enlightenment we must base ourselves on morality, which serves as the foundation of our practicing the teachings, and then we should develop single-pointed concentration and the wisdom realizing emptiness.

Here if you have some understanding or insight, or some understanding of selflessness or emptiness with the wish or aim to only overcome what is known as delusions or afflictive thoughts and emotions, then when you use that understanding merely for that purpose, you can actually reach a stage where you are completely free from samsara. Whereas in order for that wisdom to serve as a cause to reach the full enlightenment of Buddhahood, you must also be able to use that understanding to overcome what is known as the *cognitive obscurations*, or the obstacles to the omniscience of a Buddha. Thus, you should be able to do that when you have the foundational support of insight into emptiness. Then, with the help of bodhicitta and the understanding of emptiness on the basis of the foundation of morality, you will be able to reach the complete enlightenment of Buddhahood. These different defilements that are within our mind, the delusions, negative thoughts, or destructive emotions, and also the cognitive obscurations are mentioned. You should not be satisfied only with studying a very few texts. You may study one text and think that with regard to the presentation or explanation of these delusions and cognitive obscurations it may be such and such, but then when you encounter other texts, you might not understand them very well. So you have to actually study the classical texts written by great Indian masters who followed the Chittamatra or Mind Only school of philosophy as well as the texts written by Madhyamaka masters. Within the Madhyamaka masters, there are also, of course, the Swatantrika Madhyamakas and also Prasangika Madhyamakas. Within the Madhyamakas, there are in Tibet what are termed as higher and lower philosophical traditions.

You have to be able to, and you must, study all these different philosophical positions found in the texts written by great Indian masters who followed different philosophical traditions. Within Buddhism, for example, you cannot just rely on a single text and say "this is the position of this philosophical school." And so Master Tsongkhapa himself has said that he actually was not satisfied with a partial study or a rough studying of the different texts written by these great Indian masters who are called the Six Ornaments or sublime masters, but instead he actually studied in great detail thoroughly all the different philosophical texts written by these great masters. Likewise, we should also follow his example and study the different texts written by other Indian masters, such as Bhavaviveka and so forth, and gain a very broad knowledge of the philosophical traditions of ancient Indian Buddhist thought and also non-Buddhist thought rather than only basing our knowledge on the study of the text called the *Presentation of Tenets*. For example, there is one text written by one Master Upa Losel. He has written a text on philosophical systems, and studying these would help you see things in a critical way and not be satisfied with just a few words or a few explanations. You should read these texts and then analyze them and also try to compare and contrast their positions and explanations with others. This way will be very helpful for you to broaden your knowledge and experience.

The next verse, "Although you train in renunciation and the mind of enlightenment, without wisdom which realizes the ultimate reality, you cannot cut the root of cyclic existence, therefore, strive to understand dependent arising," shows the reason why we must cultivate the wisdom realizing selflessness. Master Tsongkhapa here uses the term *dependent arising* (meaning dependent origination) and he doesn't refer to understanding emptiness or selflessness.

So, you might think that dependent origination simply means things that we see conventionally and wonder how this can actually overcome clinging to dependence on these negative thoughts and emotions and from wrong views. Here what you must understand is that when Master Tsongkhapa uses the term *dependent arising*, he is referring to the subtle understanding of dependence, because when you have the subtle understanding of things that are dependent on other factors, then this will, in turn, bring about your certainty into the empty nature of phenomena, that things are empty of independent existence. This insight into emptiness will help you gain deeper understanding or an insight into the subtle dependent nature of things. They will be mutually complementary. Usually I refer to this subtle dependency of things as the *suchness of dependent origination*; what that means is that things are merely designated, that they are nominally existent. And so that is the subtle interdependent nature of things. When you understand how things are dependently designated in a very subtle way, that they are nominally existent only, then you are able to understand how things have no self-existence nature or essence in themselves; and therefore the text says: "strive to understand dependent arising." And then the next verse says: "One who sees the infallible cause and effect of all phenomena in cyclic existence and peace, and destroys all focuses of apprehension, has entered into the path which pleases the Buddha." Here we find the reference to cause and effect, the infallibility of cause and effect. Of course, when you think about the relationship between cause and effect, you are able to see that causes bring about their effect or result, and therefore effects are dependent on their causes. However, we don't get the idea of the fact that the causes are also dependent on or related to the effects, conditioned by the effects as well. And if you think carefully, the mere fact that we can say something is a cause is because of the effect that it brings about, and what we have to understand is that the cause has its identity contingent upon the effect that it brings about. In this way, you have to see that cause and effect are also mutually dependent, related, or contingent.

When we think about and have a sense of an effect, we think about something that is to come in the future, but then we are not able to see the cause and the relatedness of the cause to its effect. And so this is how you should look at causes also being related and contingent on effects; the very nature of the cause is because of its effect. Similarly, we can talk about an action—that action involves a doer, the action itself, and the agent—and then how the action is done. So, all these things—the object upon whom the action is being performed, the actor, and the action itself—all these are interrelated, interdependent, and similarly, this is the case with objects and their perceptions or conceptions, or the valid cognitions that see them. They are also mutually dependent, and so things have to be seen in terms of mutual dependence in this way. If you were to posit that things can be formed, and if you actually think that there must be some essence in things that we must be able to find through analysis, then actually, there is nothing that we can find.

If you hold on to the kind of view that there is any essence whatsoever in phenomena that is objectively there, this is not realistic in the world. Many of the happenings in the world and different processes will subsequently not be compatible with such a view, and so you will have lots of difficulties holding onto this view—that there is some kind of essence in things that are in fact only designated. Therefore you should understand that things are designated through dependence or through designation and that they are nominally existent. If you could read Chapter 24 of Master Nagarjuna's treatise, *Fundamental Wisdom of the Middle Way*, you would find this point very clearly explained there. When you understand the infallibility of the law of causality or karmic causality, what you will also find is that because things are brought about through causes and conditions, it is feasible to see that they are related or dependent on other factors. In turn, you will gain insight into emptiness as well.

On the basic understanding of the infallibility of causality, which is the apparent nature of things, you will be able to see the empty nature of things via the so-called appearance. How things exist in terms of causality will bring about the understanding of the empty nature of things, and that in turn should actually bring about the deeper understanding of how things appear to us and how things are like an illusion. If you are not yet able to complement these two, that is the subject of the next verse: "Appearances are infallible dependent arising; and emptiness is the understanding that is free of assertions. As long as these two are seen as distinct, you have not yet realized the intent of the Buddha." *Distinct* here means that you do not have understanding of these two being able to complement each other, but they happen rather alternately. As long as you are in that situation, you have not yet realized Buddha's intent, which is that when these two realizations are simultaneous, the mere sight of dependent origination concurrently destroys all roots of grasping through definite discernment. "When you understand that emptiness arises in the form of cause and effect, you are not captivated by the view of extremes."

Then finally Master Tsongkhapa actually exhorts his disciples with this concluding verse. He says, "Oh! Child, once you have realized the points of the Three Principles of the Path, seek solitude and cultivate strong determination, and quickly reach the final goal!" He shows this path that he taught to his disciple Ngawang Drakpa to exhort him to apply himself to the teaching and seek solitude. Having listened to the teaching from such masters, you develop understanding based on listening or hearing the teaching. On the basis of that, you should give thought to the teaching again and again so that you generate or develop this wisdom or understanding based on analyzing, thinking, or reflecting on the teaching. Then, having done that, you must have this deep certainty in applying the teaching in meditation. Eventually, you develop the wisdom that arises through meditation or deeper insight. Within this experience, of course, there are experiences that come about with some effort, and then once you have put in effort over a period of time, it develops into a stage where you have this meditative experience effortlessly.

Of course, if you do give thought to the teachings, you will be able to make some transformation within. You don't have to wait until you are able to go into meditation, but even if you have a very good or correct understanding of the teaching, that will in itself bring about some change in you. I can tell you this based on my own experience. When you are able to make some transformation within by giving thought to the teachings, then you will also have a happy life. There is this onset of happiness in your life even if you may be surrounded by very difficult circumstances. Deep within, you will not be swept away by these circumstances, but rather you will be able to maintain your happiness.

You should actually draw this wisdom or understanding based on your study and listening to the teaching; then develop a hundred percent certainty in the teaching through reflection using your reason and logic. Bringing about this certainty through logic is called *reflection*.

In my own case, I have applied myself in meditation for over seventy years, and because of this constant effort that I have been putting in to my practice, when I think about the fact that things are dependently originated, there is this sense I have of things being like an illusion. Here, of course, I am not making any claims to having real experience of emptiness or bodhicitta. However poor I may be in my spiritual experience, I can assure you that I have had a taste of the teaching of Buddha in terms of emptiness and bodhicitta. So you also, especially the younger generation, should give thought to these teachings, and not just the teachings, but keep thinking over and over about these teachings and the principles of dependent origination and make some effort. If you wish to make some transformation within, you must make an effort. If you find it impossible to do that, then when you have difficulties, either you just go to sleep, or you will take to drinking, but these will not really help. If you really give thought to the teachings carefully and deeply, I can assure you that transformation will happen in you. You should be determined to cultivate bodhicitta and an understanding of the wisdom of emptiness, which are the essence of the teaching of Buddha.

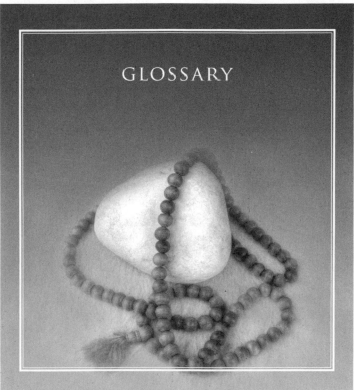

GLOSSARY

Afflictions: A class of dissonant mental states, including both thoughts and emotions, that have their root in ignorance.

Aggregate: Five psychophysical components that constitute the mind-body complex; that is, of form, feelings, perception, motivational tendencies, and consciousness.

Antidote: Just as a specific medicine is an antidote for a specific illness, in training the mind, mental states like compassion and loving-kindness are seen as antidotes against a negative mental state.

Arhat: Foe destroyer, a highly evolved spiritual person who has eliminated all the afflictions.

Aryadeva: A disciple of Acharya Nagarjuna.

Asanga: Served as the Abbot of Nalanda for twelve years, caring for the great monastic university and upholding the doctrine of Buddha.

Attachment: The three poisons of the mind are attachment, delusion, and aversion. If attachment is taken to an extreme, it becomes insatiable craving and can also be seen as biased love.

Awakening mind: An altruistic intention to attain Buddhahood for the benefit of all beings.

Awareness: Encompasses knowing and being aware of all knowing and being aware of all experiences of consciousness. It is also viewed as intelligence and knowledge-based discipline.

Bhavaviveka: A disciple of Acharya Nagarjuna.

Bodhicitta: This is the mind of enlightenment. On the relative level, it is the wish to attain Buddhahood for the sake of all beings, as well as the practice of the path of love, compassion, and the six transcendent perfections necessary for achieving that goal. On the absolute level, it is the direct insight into the ultimate nature of reality.

Bodhisattva: A spiritual practitioner dedicated to the cultivation of bodhicitta or the altruistic intention to attain enlightenment. The basic commitment is to work for others and remain purposely within cyclic existence instead of simply seeking freedom from suffering for oneself.

Buddha: The One who is awakened or enlightened. A fully awakened being trains his or her mind by walking on the bodhisattva path, finally realizes his or her potential for complete enlightenment, and eliminates all the obscurations to true knowledge and liberation. A Buddha's characteristic features are found in his or her body, speech, mind, attributes, and activities.

Buddhahood: When one has attained total freedom from karmically conditioned existence and fully realized or manifested all aspects of Buddha/body/speech/mind/attributes/activities.

Cessation: The end of all suffering usually references the third of the four noble truths—the truth of the cessation of suffering and its causes.

Chandrakirti: A Buddhist scholar who composed the *Entry into the Middle Way*, which clarifies the profound and extensive view of Nagarjuna.

Compassion: This is referred to as a *great compassion*, which is a totally unbiased mind that wishes for the liberation of all sentient beings from suffering and cannot be mistaken for pity, which may have a connotation of superiority toward the object of compassion.

Conditioned existence: A synonym for *cyclic existence*, the way we are trapped in an endless round of rebirths due to the continual ripening of causes and conditions of negative karmic imprints.

Consciousness: Refers to a nonmaterial capacity to illuminate and bring to awareness both the objective and subjective reality. Consciousness has the quality of luminosity and clarity. According to Buddhist philosophy, there are many types of consciousness.

Cyclic existence: Life that is conditioned by dissonant mental states and the karmic imprints characterized by suffering in a cycle of life, death, and rebirth, in which the six classes of sentient beings rotate.

Dependent origination: Or *pratityasamutpada* as it is known in Sanskrit. This is the most fundamental metaphysical view in Buddhism. This principle asserts that everything that exists is dependent on other factors. In other words, multiple causes and conditions create things and events. There are twelve links of dependent origination: ignorance, motivational tendencies, consciousness, name and form, sensory activity fields, contact, sensation, attachment, grasping, rebirth, birth, aging, and death. All these links are interconnected and each component of the chain contributes to this endless ignorance-filled cycle.

Dharma: This means *to hold* or *to maintain*. In Buddhism it denotes teachings or doctrines. After Buddha's enlightenment, Buddha's first sermon was called "Turning the Wheel of Dharma." In general Dharma also refers to one's spiritual practice, specifically Buddha's teachings, which protect from suffering and lead to liberation and full enlightenment.

Dharmakirti: A scholar who composed the continuous praise to Heruka and gained complete mastery of the methods of refutation. He built a temple in the land of Kalinga.

Dignaga: A disciple of Vasubandu who surpassed even his own teacher in logic.

Emptiness: The ultimate nature of reality or the absence of inherent existence and self-identity with reality and all phenomena. Suchness, actual reality, and ultimate truth are synonymous. Thus, at an internal and external level, all things and events do not possess any independent, intrinsic reality that defines their essence.

Enlightenment: The ultimate goal one aspires to on the Buddhist path. One is considered enlightened or awakened when one has succeeded in purifying afflictive emotions as well as obstruction to knowledge. A person who has attained enlightenment is called a Buddha or the awakened one.

Equanimity: A state of even-mindedness, an unbiased mind toward others. Normally, one's attitude toward other persons is strongly affected by erasing them as friends, enemies, or strangers. Hence, one regards others as completely equal and gets rid of partiality toward them with equanimity. One has the same attitude toward friends, enemies, and strangers.

The five inner and outer elements: These five elements consist of earth, water, fire, air, and space. The five inner elements compose our bodies, whereas the five outer elements compose our universe.

The four noble truths: These are the subject of the first discourse given by Sakyamuni Buddha in Sarnath following his attainment of Buddhahood in Bodh Gaya. The four truths are (a) truth of suffering, (b) the truth of its origins, (c) the truth of its cessation, and (d) the truth of the path leading to such cessation. The entire structure of the path to Buddhahood is built on these four truths, and thus, they hold the key to success in one's spiritual practice.

The four reliances: (1) One should not rely on the teacher but on the teaching; (2) one should not rely on the words but on the meaning expressed; (3) one should rely on the definitive meaning and not the provisional meaning; and finally (4) one should rely on transcendent wisdom of deep experience and not merely on knowledge.

The four seals: In order for a school to be Buddhist, it must accept the following four seals: (1) All composite phenomena are impermanent. (2) All contaminated things and events are unsatisfactory. (3) All phenomena are empty and selfless. (4) Nirvana is true peace.

Gampopa: The most famous disciple of Milarepa and founder of the Kagyapa monastic order.

Highest yoga tantra: Also known as anuttarayoga tantra. The highest among four classes of tantra; the other are action (kriya), performance (charya), and yoga tantra.

Impermanence: This is one of the marks of casually conditioned phenomena along with suffering and the absence of self identity. It alludes to the momentary changing nature of things that are always fluid and in flux.

Inherent existence: Objectively phenomena are attributed with an inherent existence in their own right and of themselves. They are seen as independent of any other phenomena such as conception and labeling.

Kadampa: The first schools of the new tradition, which followed the teachings of Atisha. These schools stressed compassion, study, and pure discipline.

Karma: A dynamic relationship between actions and results. Physical, verbal, and mental causality create psychological imprints and tendencies within the mind as a result of one's actions. Hence, a casual chain is maintained within the mental continuum that can be traced in present and future lives, and karma ripens as and when it encounters the approximate circumstances and conditions.

Lama: Venerable teacher or guru—someone who is weighty because he or she is a master of the inner world and is supreme and unsurpassed. To be a lama, specific qualifications are necessary. These may differ according to the level of spiritual practice.

Liberation: This deals with the freedom from cyclic existence—the cycle of birth, death, and rebirth—and freedom from all forms of physical and mental suffering.

Mahayana: Also known as the greater vehicle, Mahayana is known in terms of its motivation; that is, the practitioner of this path emphasizes altruism and keeps the liberation of all sentient beings as the principal objective.

Mandala: This connotes a circle, wheel, circumference, totality, and assembly of the literary corpus. In a more general usage, this term points to the central and peripheral deities described in Tantric texts. The mandala generally represents a perfected state of being and perception encompassing all phenomena.

Mantra: An abbreviation of two syllables: mana and traya, mind and protection. Mantra can be considered as the protection of the mind from deluded states of existence so the full expression of Buddha nature is not inhibited. Mantra also refers to the pure sound that is the perfected speech of an enlightened being.

Meditation: Through a disciplined mental process, the ability to cultivate familiarity with a chosen object, whether it is external or internal. There are two main types of meditation: the calm-abiding, which deals with stability and the single-pointedness of the mind, and the other penetrative insights, which emphasize analysis and discrimination.

Mindfulness: Enables the mind to maintain its attention on a referent object, making it familiar, and creating the ability to retain its imprint within the memory for future recollection. This practice also counteracts forgetfulness.

Nagarjuna, Acharya: A Buddhist scholar who became the Abbot of Nalanda University.

Nalanda: The birthplace near Rajgir of the Buddha's disciple Sariputra, which much later, starting at the time of the Gupta kings (5th century) became one of the great centers of learning in Buddhist India.

Negativity: Results in creating a momentum toward a less-favorable rebirth within cyclic existence because it arises from the performance of nonvirtuous past actions, along with the negative obscurations and their habitual tendencies based on delusion, attachment, and aversion.

Nirvana: The permanent cessation of all suffering and the dissonant mental states that create suffering, along with all misapprehensions related to the nature of emptiness. It is viewed as the antithesis of samsara.

The noble eightfold path: Also referred to as the *fourth noble truth*. Used to overcome suffering the noble eightfold path has been suggested. This path consists of the right view, right intention, right speech, right action, right livelihood, right effort, right mindfulness, and right meditative stabilization.

Omniscience: Indicates the all-knowing, pristine cognition of the Buddha. It is understood in terms of a direct and simultaneous perception of the dual aspects of reality, that is, of the phenomenal aspects and their ultimate nature.

Purification: The practice of cleansing your past negative karma.

Refuge: In this state, one entrusts one's spiritual growth and well-being to the three precious jewels: Buddha, Dharma, and Sangha. These are also known as the objects of refuge, and the nature of refuge sought for each of the three is different. In the Buddha, guidance on a correct path to Buddhahood is sought; in Dharma, the sacred teachings lead to realizations of the path; and in Sangha (Monastic Community) perfect companionship on the path to Buddhahood is sought.

Renunciation: A mental attitude that does not cling to all worldly attributes such as wealth, fame, position, and the thought of a favorable rebirth in a future life. One is also not merely separate from objects of desire but has a mental quality of liberation, which is free from even the slightest degree of craving for mundane values.

Sangha: The third object of refuge. This generally refers to the community of monks or nuns. Absolute

Sangha are those who have directly realized emptiness, whereas relative Sangha are ordained monks and nuns. The Buddhist Sangha began with the ordination of a group of five monks to whom the Buddha delivered his first sermon.

Selflessness: The lack of inherent existence both in mental and physical phenomena. In addition to being an absence of an independently existing self or "I," selflessness embraces all the physical and mental realities. Selflessness is equated with emptiness and speaks of the selflessness of a person and the selflessness of phenomena.

Shantarakshita: Scholar of the Tripitaka and profound stages of the path in accordance with Nagarjuna's view. He taught the ten virtuous actions and the twelve links of dependent origination.

Six consciousnesses: Also known as the six gatherings of consciousness, the gathering of a sense of object, a sense organ, and of a consciousness. The six consciousnesses are vision, hearing, smell, taste, touch, and mental consciousness.

Six perfections: Longevity, good health, success, and happiness in Buddhism are dependent on kindness and a good heart. Thus, the bodhisattva clearly needs to practice the six perfections: generosity, ethical discipline, tolerance, joyous effort, concentration, and wisdom.

Six realms of existence: These are hell, hungry ghosts, animal, human, god, and demigod. The six realms of existence are predominantly caused by a particular mental poison hell (anger) of animals (ignorance), of humans (desire), of pretas (miserliness), of demigods (jealousy), and of gods (pride). The karma of beings produces these deluded perceptions.

Suffering: Used in a broad sense to include both physical sensations and mental experiences; that is, all the unsatisfactory experiences of life in cyclic existence. There are three kinds of suffering: (1) the suffering of suffering, (2) the suffering of change, and (3) the suffering of pervasive conditioning. Suffering also has been identified as the first of the four noble truths. One can bring an end to cyclic existence by eliminating suffering by adopting the entire path of Buddhism.

Sutrayana: The Sutra vehicle or the path to awakening that relies upon the philosophical, ethical, and meditative systems belonging to the Sutra texts or the esoteric discoveries of the Buddha.

Tantra: The Sanskrit word *Tantra* means a "continuum" or an "unbroken stream" flowing from the fundamental ignorance to enlightenment.

Ten nonvirtuous actions : These actions are associated with body, speech, and mind. The three physical nonvirtues are killing, stealing, and adultery. The four verbal nonvirtues are lying—deceiving others through spoken words or gestures—divisiveness, harsh talk, and senseless speech. The three mental nonvirtues are covetousness, harmful intent, and wrong view.

Theravada: Buddhist spiritual paths that emphasize individual liberation from the sufferings of cyclic existence; also called the lesser vehicle.

The three jewels of Buddhism: (1) The Buddha Jewel refers to the enlightened teacher, or one's own future state of enlightenment; (2) the Dharma Jewel points to the teachings and realizations that lead to happiness, liberation, and enlightenment; and (3) the Sangha Jewel deals with the spiritual community of those on the Buddhist path.

The three kayas: Also known as the doctrine of three bodies, which presents the Mahayana understanding of the nature of Buddhahood. The Dharmakaya, or reality body, is the ultimate expanse that is the final reality of a Buddha's awakening; indeed, it is the ultimate mind of the Buddha. The Sambhogakaya, or enjoyment body, is the form of enlightened mind that remains in the perfect realm of existence; this subtle form is perceptible only to highly advanced practitioners. The Nirmanakaya, or emanation body, is the form of Buddha that is visible to ordinary sentient beings.

Three levels of consciousness: These levels deal with the subtlety of consciousness—the gross, the subtle, and the very subtle states of mind. The gross consciousness depends upon the gross physical aggregates and can be linked with waking states. The subtle mind is linked with dreaming or intermediate states, and the very subtle consciousness is associated with deep sleep or a continuum of clear light of death.

Three meanings: The three kinds of meanings to be achieved: the highest, middle, and the lowest. The highest meaning is to reach full enlightenment, Buddhahood, in this life. The middle meaning is to achieve self-liberation from samsaric fears and sufferings. The lowest meaning is to try to obtain a peaceful mind, to solve one's inner problems, and not to be reborn in the lower realms.

Tripitaka: The three collections of the Buddha's teachings: *Vinaya*, *Sutra*, and *Abhidharma*. The Vajrayana teachings are sometimes considered a fourth pitaka. Tripitaka means "three baskets," so called because the palm-leaf folios on which the scriptures were originally written were collected and stored in baskets.

Tsongkhapa: A great Tibetan teacher and founder of the Geluk tradition (1357–1419).

Two truths: All Buddhist schools formulate their ontology within the framework of two truths: the conventional or relative truth, and the ultimate truth. Ultimate truth is defined as a synonym of phenomena, whereas the conventional truth is experienced through our perceptions as an empirical aspect of reality.

Vajrayana: *Vajra* has the connotation of inseparability of method and wisdom and also the inseparability of body, speech, and mind. *Yana* is path. *Vajrayana* is the path that tries to achieve these two inseparabilities with its unique methods based on the principle of the three paths as cultivated in Sutrayana—renunciation, bodhicitta, and the wisdom of emptiness. This is also known as *Mantrayana*.

Wisdom: A mind that correctly understands its object and eliminates doubts. Wisdom also implies all aspects of the path to enlightenment associated with the development of the realization of emptiness.

Yidam: A deity representing enlightenment, in a male or female, peaceful or wrathful form, corresponding to one's individual nature. The yidam is the source of accomplishments.

ACKNOWLEDGMENTS

My greatest debt is to His Holiness the Dalai Lama for the crucial role he has played in my life as a mind-transformer. His very presence touches the core of my being, and he inspires many with his scholarship, simplicity, spontaneity, patience, and a kind heart. I value this opportunity to put his thoughts together in a subjectively systematic manner.

Thanks are due to Geshe Lhakdor, director of the Library of Tibetan Works and Archives in Dharamsala for allowing me to use some of His Holiness's writings and teachings. Geshe Dorji Damdul, director, Tibet House, New Delhi has also been a constant source of emotional and intellectual support for my work. I am grateful to him. I cannot forget to appreciate the cooperation of the members of the Private Office of His Holiness and my friends and colleagues at both Tushita and Jawaharlal Nehru University for their generosity and warmth.

Finally, I wish to acknowledge the loving presence of my family, the Pauls and Mehtas in the United States, for all their encouragement and universal tolerance.

BIBLIOGRAPHY

His Holiness the Dalai Lama. *Activating Bodhicitta and a Meditation*. Dharamsala, India: Library of Tibetan Works and Archives (LTWA), 2006.

———. *Awakening the Mind, Lightening the Heart*. Edited by Donald S. Lopez, Jr. Dharamsala, India: LTWA, 2008.

———. *Cultivating a Daily Meditation*. Dharamsala, India: LTWA, 1991.

———. *Four Essential Buddhist Commentaries*. Dharamsala, India: LTWA, 1993.

———. *The Joy of Living and Dying in Peace*. Edited by Donald S. Lopez Jr. Dharamsala, India: LTWA, 2008.

———. *The Key to Madhya Mika*. Dharamsala, India: LTWA, 1976.

————. *Opening the Mind and Generating a Good Heart.* Translated by Tsepak Rigzin and Jeremy Russell. Dharamsala, India: LTWA, 1995.

————. *Universal Responsibility and the Good Heart.* Dharamsala, India: LTWA, 1980.

————.*The Way to Freedom.* Edited by Donald S. Lopez Jr. Dharamsala, India: LTWA, 2008.

His Holiness the Dalai Lama and Thubten Chodron. *Buddhism: One Teacher, Many Traditions.* Boston: Wisdom Publications, 2014: 275–276.

His Holiness the Dalai Lama and Renuka Singh, ed. *Many Ways to Nirvana.* New Delhi, India: Viking/Penguin, 2004.

His Holiness the Dalai Lama and Renuka Singh. *The Transformed Mind.* New Delhi, India: Viking/Penguin, 1999.

Jinpa, Geshe Thubten. *The World of Tibetan Buddhism*. Boston: Wisdom Publications, 1995.

Nagarjuna. "Fundamental Wisdom of the Middle Way." In *Emptiness, A Study in Religious Meaning*, translated by F. J. Streng. Nashville, N.Y: Abingdon Press, 1967.

Singh, Renuka, ed. *The Path of the Buddha: Writings on Contemporary Buddhism*. New Delhi, India: Penguin, 2004.

——, ed. *The Path to Tranquility*. New Delhi, India: Viking, 1998.

——. *Women Reborn: An Exploration of the Spirituality of Urban Indian Women*. New Delhi, India: Penguin, 1997.